OF THE SOMME

Martin Marix Evans

PHOENIX ILLUSTRATED

Dedication
*To Leo, who started it,
Tonie and Valmai, who pointed
the way, and to Gillian, Louise
and Polly, who tolerated the
consequences.*

Copyright © Martin Marix Evans, 1996
Martin Marix Evans has asserted his right to
be identified as the Author of this work

First published in 1996 by
George Weidenfeld & Nicolson Ltd

This paperback edition first published in 1998 by
Phoenix Illustrated
Orion Publishing Group,
Orion House,
5, Upper St. Martin's Lane
London WC2H 9EA

British Library Cataloguing-in-Publication Data
A catalogue record for this book is available from
the British Library

ISBN: 0753804891

Printed and bound in Italy

Designed by Adrian Hodgkins Design
Typesetting by White Horse Graphics
Map by Micro Map

NOTE ON THE MAPS

Contemporary Ordnance Survey maps are used to illustrate the British knowledge of the battle front at the time. The grid lines are marked as continuous lines at intervals of 1,000 yards (914 metres), and as dotted lines at half that distance. Each block of 30 squares has an identifying letter, and each square within that block a number. References in the text use this system giving the relevant square in brackets, except that where the initial letter is not visible on the detail reproduced, it is omitted. For security, British trenches were not usually marked. Annotations and markings on the maps were made at the time, and some of the maps bear obvious signs of wear and tear. The maps are from the archives of the Tank Museum at Bovington in Dorset.

ACKNOWLEDGEMENTS

The constructive and patient assistance of Marie-Pascale Prévost-Bault of the Historial de la Grande Guerre, Péronne; David Fletcher of the Tank Museum, Bovington, Dorset, and his former colleague, Graham Holmes; and the staff of the Department of Photographs, Imperial War Museum, London are gratefully acknowledged. A particular debt of gratitude is owed to Toby Buchan for his work on the script.

The illustrations in this book are subject to copyright and are reproduced by kind permission of the Historial de la Grande Guerre (HGG), the Trustees of the Imperial War Museum (IWM), the National Archive, Washington, DC (NA), the Tank Museum (TM), and Popperfoto (P). The modern colour photographs are by the author. Ordnance Survey maps of the battlefields are Crown Copyright.

The quotations from John Masefield are reproduced by permission of the Society of Authors as the literary representative of the Estate of John Masefield. The literary executors of certain authors quoted have not been traced at the time of going to press and the author will be grateful for any information as to their identity and whereabouts.

The following illustrations are uncaptioned. Endpapers: Australian troops working along an assault trench on Mont St Quentin, near Péronne, September 1918 (P). Half-title: Canadian troops attacking on the Somme (TM). Title: Heavy artillery on the Somme (TM 1449-B-5). Pages 16/17: British troops attack (P). Pages 34/35: Heavy artillery in front of Mametz, July 1916 (P). Pages 66/67: Tanks and troops in front of Bellicourt, 29 September 1918 (TM 319/94). Page 96: Flat Iron Copse Cemetery, Mametz Wood (MFME).

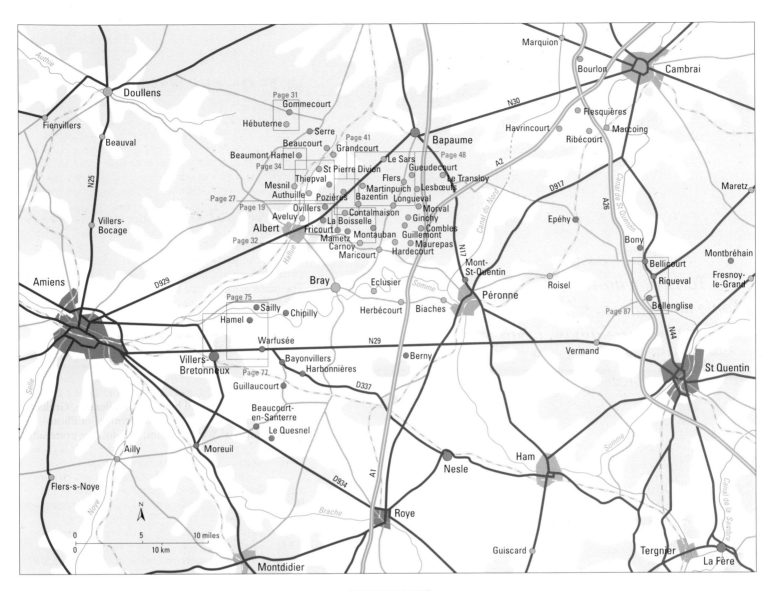

CONTENTS

PRELUDE
TO THE
SOMME

The war had already lasted two years before the Somme saw substantial action. Much had been learned – but not enough.

Below: The massive steel observation dome of Fort Vaux broods over the shell-pocked country above Verdun. (MFME A/V 2/27)

WHEN THE First World War broke out in August 1914 the two principal adversaries in the West, the Germans and the French, thought the war would soon be over. The Germans had complete confidence in the Schlieffen Plan, the strategy of sweeping through Belgium to take Paris from the north, while the French relied equally on Plan XVII, which involved a strike to the east through the lands lost in the Franco-Prussian War, Lorraine and Alsace. Neither succeeded. The French were thrown back towards Verdun and the Germans halted on the Marne, just short of their objective. As each side tried to outflank the other the front line extended south-east and north-west. In Flanders the comparatively tiny British Expeditionary Force (BEF), added its skills to those of the huge conscript army of France to halt the rush of the Germans towards the English Channel. In October, in a desperate action in front of Ypres, the BEF secured the northern end of what became known as the Western Front. From the Belgian coast to the Swiss border the opposing forces dug in, and in the following months created a complex of trenches and defences that ran across half of Europe.

A static war was something for which the generals on both sides were unprepared. Theirs was largely an experience of wars of manoeuvre, of

Above: French soldiers, wearing the Adrien helmets introduced in 1916, test firing a captured German Maxim machine-gun. (HGG)

battles against relatively unsophisticated opponents in which they employed combinations of infantry and cavalry movement. The impact of new weapons on military thinking was still superficial, although the immediate practical use of such weapons was understood. They had at their disposal artillery of a power formerly undreamed of: light and medium field guns, heavy howitzers, and even huge naval guns mounted on railway trucks, capable of firing immense explosive shells with uncanny accuracy for many miles. Indeed, so impressed were they that reliance on artillery power and an over-estimation of what it could achieve led to serious tactical errors. It was, however, the invention of an American (though he became a naturalised British subject), Hiram Maxim, that made the trench system so easy to defend. He devised a gun which harnessed the recoil automatically to eject the spent cartridge, chamber a new one, close the breech block, and fire the weapon. From this the British developed the Vickers medium machine-gun, the Germans the Maxim and the French the St-Étienne. All three were tripod mounted, had water-cooled barrels, and were capable of firing 500 rifle-calibre rounds per minute. This rate of fire was somewhat academic since heat would jam or destroy the weapon long before such a rate could be attained (the reason machine-gunners are taught to fire short bursts); besides, the Vickers and the Maxim ammunition belts held 250 rounds and the St-Étienne's held 300, but all were capable of laying down a withering hail of bullets. Their weight limited their mobility – the Vickers weighed in at 68 pounds (30.8kg), and the Maxim at a massive 115 pounds (52kg) – but for beating off an attack by massed infantry in the open they could scarcely be bettered.

Lighter air-cooled machine-guns, such as the Lewis with which the British forces were equipped, were suited to more mobile use and also to mounting in aircraft. Like the Vickers, this gun (the 1911 invention of Colonel Isaac Newton Lewis of the US Army, though his country declined to adopt it until after the war had started) had the advantage of using .303 ammunition, the same as the British Lee-Enfield rifle, fed from a 47-round drum magazine mounted on top of the action. This simplified the problem of supplying ammunition to troops in the line. The Lewis's rate of fire was of the order of 450-500 rounds per minute, and though it was prone to stoppages, it became a standard infantry weapon. By the end of the war the Germans had introduced the first sub-machine-guns for use by 'storm troop' attack divisions.

A further incentive to static war was the overall situation at the end of 1914. The Germans had seized most of Belgium and a great slice of northern France before the over-extension of their supply lines and the stiffening resistance of the Allies brought the advance to a halt. Germany's objective for the time being was to hold the territory occupied. The British and French, in order to gain time in which to recoup their strength, also needed to hold where they were, but with a view eventually to ejecting the invader. German trenches were therefore built to last, while the Allies needed adequate, defensible cover essentially temporary in conception. In all this the cavalry, helpless against both artillery and machine-gun fire, was largely irrelevant.

The battles of 1915, Second Ypres, Neuve Chapelle and Loos among them, were costly but did nothing to break the stalemate or give either side advantage. The British professional army had, however, been reduced to a mere rump, capable of holding its line, but until reinforced by new recruits, no great threat. It was also clear that infantry attacks on prepared positions were not the answer, and the Germans needed a new idea if they were to prevail.

THE BLACK HOLE OF VERDUN

General Erich von Falkenhayn, the then Chief of the German General Staff, knew that the French were more highly motivated than their allies. It was their soil that had been violated, their homeland that had been occupied. Further, the French had many more men under arms and had suffered far greater losses than the British. Perhaps, Falkenhayn reasoned, the war could be won before the British could build their strength and before the troops now coming from the Colonies and Dominions of the British Empire could take the field in large numbers. The destruction of the French Army would 'knock [England's] best sword out of her hand'.

The target was selected with care; it had to be one the French would give everything to defend. The huge forts above Verdun were to be his killing ground.

The French Commander-in-Chief, General Joseph Joffre, was in fact willing to yield this ground; strategically it was of no importance to his campaign. Politically, however, the Verdun fortifications, created after the humiliation of the French defeat in the Franco-Prussian War of 1870, were of enormous symbolic significance, and the soldier was overruled by his political masters. Thus when, on 21 February 1916, the 1,400 guns of the Germans opened fire on Verdun, the French resisted. The prevailing defensive philosophy that guided them was 'l'attaque à'outrance' – attack to the bitter end; any position

Above: Defensive positions were strengthened with barbed-wire entanglements to slow or halt attackers and make them easy prey for rifle or machine-gun fire. These French soldiers are constructing wooden supports for their wire and thus a barrier that could be moved into position quickly. Specially designed metal stakes secured entanglements constructed free of enemy harrassment. (HGG)

Right: A German soldier in an observation post on the Somme front. The metal shield set into the sand-bagged parapet offers cover from view as well as cover from fire. The old-style helmet, replaced with the familiar coal-scuttle steel design in 1916, was a souvenir highly prized by British troops. (P)

taken by the enemy must be counter-attacked at all costs and regained. Falkenhayn relied on this to tempt the French to bleed themselves white at Verdun.

To some extent Falkhayn had misjudged. Given the low priority accorded to the position by Joffre, the defences were lightly manned and many of the guns of the forts had been withdrawn. Success came more easily than expected, drawing the Germans into the hand-to-hand fighting the original plan had intended to avoid. By 25 February Fort Douaumont had fallen to the Germans, taken by nine men of the 24th Brandenburg

Left: Aerial photography gave mappers excellent reference for the preparation of detailed trench plans. This picture of trenches at La Bassée, south-west of Lille, was taken in January 1916 and shows the crenellated pattern of a fighting trench, which reduced the effect of shell or grenade bursts or of enfilading fire along the position. Communication trenches have less pronounced twists and turns. (TM 5086/D6)

Regiment who climbed through an undefended embrasure and overwhelmed the fifty-seven men inside. The expected counter-attack did not come. The French Second Army commander here, General Philippe Pétain, who had been brought in to command at Verdun when the German assault started, husbanded his soldiers' lives and his more cautious approach drew the Germans in. Nevertheless, by March France had suffered 89,000 casualties and the Germans 81,000. Here was France, heroically defending her homeland, and what were the British doing?

As the hills above the little town in the Meuse were ground into a wilderness of mud and blood, and as French reinforcements were swallowed up in the apparently never-ending maelstrom, the demands on the British Commander-in-Chief, General Sir Douglas Haig, to relieve the pressure by launching an attack in the north-west became irresistible.

Any attack, anywhere, so long as it drew off the power of the Germans at Verdun, and it must be soon, by the end of June at the latest. Haig agreed, although he would have preferred to have until September to build up his forces and complete their training. The waterlogged terrain of Flanders was uninviting and the southern end of the British line, where it met the French line in Picardy, was therefore chosen. The battle would take place where the British line, running roughly north-south, was bisected by the River Somme.

While Haig made his preparations the horror at Verdun continued. On 19 April Pétain was promoted to command the Central Army Group and General Robert Nivelle replaced him at Verdun. His style was much more to the public taste; dramatic attacks and resounding utterances such as his general order of 23 June: 'Ils ne passeront pas!' – 'They shall not pass!' In fact, a corruption – the order reads 'Vous ne les laisserez passer'. More Frenchmen were poured into the battle.

The Germans attacked Fort Vaux on 1 June. Two hundred and fifty men, under the command of Major Sylvain-Eugène Raynal, defended it inch by inch. The outer defences fell on the first day, and the dogged Frenchmen were forced back though the dank passages over the next week. Their only method of communicating with the outside world was by carrier pigeon, of which they had four. Their appeals for support went unanswered and the last of the birds flew through gas clouds to headquarters on 4 June, dying on arrival. The drinking water ran out the next day, but it was not until 7 June that Raynal surrendered. It was to be in July that the Germans suffered their first reverse, at Fort Souville, and they were slowly forced back thereafter. By the end of August the French casualties at Verdun had reached

Below: French heavy artillery at Verdun. The shells for the 150-mm guns were brought up on 60-cm gauge rail trolleys. (HGG)

the incredible figure of 315,000 men killed or wounded. The German losses numbered some 261,000. Up to and during the Battle of the Somme the carnage at Verdun exerted its influence, and the scale of the French losses coloured the attitude to casualties in Picardy.

THE ARMIES ON THE SOMME

Unlike Germany and France, there was no conscription in Britain before the war. The small Regular Army was composed of full-time professionals, backed up by the part-time Territorials for home defence in Britain. The Regular Army was terribly mauled in 1914 and 1915 with the result that the Territorial Force was drawn into overseas service. The wisdom of the Secretary of State for War, Field Marshal Lord Kitchener, in appealing for fresh volunteers at the start of the war was proved. The response had been massive. These men made up the battalions of Kitchener's New Armies.

Conscription had given Germany and France a vast pool of trained manpower, ready to be called to the colours and quickly brought up to operational fitness. The volunteers who responded to Kitchener's call – and just under 2,500,000 men volunteered for the Army between August 1914 and the end of 1915 – had no such military experience. Clerks and labourers, miners and farm workers enlisted in a torrent of patriotic enthusiasm, but they knew nothing of war. What was yet more problematical was the lack of officers to lead them. Five hundred British officers of the Indian Army who happened to be in England were found, and a further 2,000 young men who had just left school or university were invited by the War Office to apply for commissions, largely untrained and inexperienced as they were. Non-commissioned officers were in equally short supply. These deficiencies were to have terrible consequences in France.

The hasty enlistment of so large a number produced strong regional characteristics in the bodies of men recruited. Whole battalions were made up of men from a single town; indeed, the objective of the recruitment drive became the formation of such units, to which the War Office made the pledge that men who worked or played together would be kept together within their battalion – the Manchester Pals, the Grimsby Chums, the Glasgow Tramways, among many others, were examples of battalions raised from single towns or trades, the latter including miners, postmen, railwaymen, sportsmen, stockbrokers. They were anything but an instant army,

for there were no uniforms for them to wear and no weapons with which to train. In spite of all these difficulties, as the months passed, disciplined units emerged from the ant-heap of volunteers. Their competence at parade-ground drills outstripped their abilities with their weapons, and their unquestioning willingness to obey orders their fighting initiative, but by the spring of 1916 General Haig had a large and growing force of new, unproven but eager and dedicated troops with which to reinforce his more experienced army in France.

Added to these were the Empire's forces – units

Below: A Canadian carries a Stokes mortar across the empty Canal du Nord during the advance of 1918. Trench mortars were designed to deliver a high-explosive shell with great accuracy. (TM 440/G3)

of the professional Indian Army; the tough and casually courageous ANZACs (that is, members of the Australia and New Zealand Army Corps), blooded at Gallipoli; the Canadians, who had already shown their mettle at Ypres, and their neighbours, the men of Newfoundland (then a self-governing British colony). Simple manpower was becoming less of a problem, but skill at arms and battlecraft were in short supply.

Supply of matériel was building as well, though not as fast as desired. The factories of Britain were turning out increasing quantities of heavy guns and ammunition, though the quality of the shells, or more precisely their detonators, was to prove poor. By the autumn Haig calculated he would have what he required, but he could not wait until then; the French had to have relief by the end of June.

The Germans held the initiative after the advance of 1914 and thus could choose their ground. In planning their lines of trenches they had known they could afford to retreat a little if necessary, so taking maximum advantage of the lie of the land to create the best defensive positions against future Allied attack.

In September 1914 the Germans had swarmed across the broad, open country to the east of Albert on the flank of the advance on Paris. On 27 September they had reached Thiepval on the edge of the Pozières Ridge, which dominates the valleys of the River Ancre to the north and the Somme to the south. The French, hurrying to contain them, reached the riverside village of Authuille below the ridge on the same day. Probing forward to locate the invaders, they saw a shadowy figure in the mist knocking in posts. They fired; he fell. Later that day they learned they had killed a fellow Frenchman, Boromée Vaquette, a farmer innocently fencing his field. He was the first victim of the war at Thiepval.

The front line stabilized here, running in the north around Gommecourt, north of the Ancre, and south just to the west of La Boisselle, Fricourt and Mametz to the marshy flood plain of the Somme. Here the French faced the Germans for more than a year. Both sides were concentrating on the battles on other fronts, so life was relatively quiet on the Somme and the Germans used the time well. The western edge of the ridge became the first line of defence, its projecting spurs fortified to cover the little valleys and the trenches sited to provide the best fields of fire. Behind this two more lines of trenches were constructed and key villages turned into strongpoints connected by a network of communication trenches. The ground was painstakingly surveyed to give the German artillery the precise range at a series of marked points along the probable routes of an attacking force. Most important of all were the deep bunkers the Germans excavated beneath their surface fortifications all along the line. In these they could survive the inevitable bombardment that would precede an Allied attack.

The British came to Picardy late in 1915, taking over the line from the overstretched French northwards from the River Somme. The Royal Flying Corps, virtually unopposed in this sector, was able to observe and photograph the long lines of chalky spoil from the German trenches, and the Ordnance Survey prepared detailed maps of the complex defences visible from the air. The deep bunkers, however, went undetected.

This was no longer the somnolent sector of 1915. The British believed in keeping the enemy on the hop with constant, small-scale probing attacks. While these revealed useful information about the obstacles they faced, they were also a strain on the troops in the front line, who had regularly to be relieved. Much of what they learned was thus wasted, while the German policy of keeping the same formations in the same positions gave them complete familiarity with their ground.

PREPARATIONS FOR BATTLE

General Haig had succeeded General Sir John French as Commander-in-Chief of the BEF in December 1915. A cavalryman with a fine career record, including service in the Boer War, he had commanded I Corps in 1914, and then First Army in 1915. Fifty-five years of age, he was a solid churchman and loyal to his subordinates; his loyalty to his seniors and, sometimes, to his peers, has often been questioned, however. He had favoured a joint operation with the French on the Somme, as had originally been planned, but the crisis at Verdun meant that the British would have to shoulder almost the entire burden of the operation, and sooner than seemed prudent. The main attack was to be undertaken by Lieutenant-General Sir Henry Rawlinson's Fourth Army, with supporting attacks by the French to the south and by Lieutenant-General Sir Edmund Allenby's Third Army, essentially mounting a diversionary action, at Gommecourt in the north.

The Fourth Army was to attack on a front from Serre in the north to Montauban in the south, to take the Pozières Ridge and so open the way for three cavalry divisions from Lieutenant-General Sir Hubert Gough's Reserve Army (renamed Fifth Army during the course of the battle) to sweep for-

ward to Bapaume. If that plan succeeded, Gough would hold the eastern flank while Rawlinson would turn his forces northwards, rolling up the German lines. Between Serre and the Gommecourt salient there was a gap of a mile which was not to be attacked, leaving Allenby's Third Army unsupported. The battle was to commence on 25 June.

Rawlinson lacked confidence in the New Army battalions. He doubted that inexperienced troops could be controlled in rushing the enemy trenches and decided that, following the example of the successful German offensive at Verdun, artillery could reduce the German trenches to ruins and wipe out their defenders, allowing his forces to advance unopposed to occupy the enemy positions. The heaviest artillery bombardment of the war, to last five days, was to achieve this, after which the troops would be able to advance in line abreast, rifles at the port, strolling forward to their objectives and mopping up the few surviving pockets of resistance. At least, that was the theory. Haig was troubled. He suggested rushing the enemy after a much briefer bombardment, thus gaining some element of surprise, and he also advocated attempting to take two lines of German trenches immediately instead of the more deliberate day-by-day schedule of bombardment followed by advance, as Rawlinson proposed. Haig also adhered to the maxim of leaving the decision to the man in command, however, and Rawlinson's plan was therefore confirmed.

The men were gathering for the 'Big Push', over half a million of them. The first attack was to be carried out almost exclusively by the British, with Indian, Australian and Canadian troops in reserve. Vast stores of munitions were assembled. Disposi-

Above: The 1st Lancashire Fusiliers fixing bayonets prior to the attack on Beaumont Hamel. Probably an exercise photographed on 30 June, the picture conveys some idea of the burden of packs and equipment attacking soldiers had to bear. (IWM Q744)

Opposite: The shell-damaged basilica of Notre-Dame des Brébières in Albert, September 1916. The church was severely damaged by German shells in January 1915, but the golden Madonna clung on at an angle and was secured by French engineers. It became an object of superstition; the Allies holding that the war would end when it fell, the Germans that those who knocked it down would lose the war. Neither proved correct. The British destroyed it by shellfire in April 1918 and a replica now crowns the restored basilica. (IWM Q855)

tions were made to deal with the casualties expected; 10,000 per day was the estimate. With the help of Royal Flying Corps observers, tasked to over-fly the German lines, the artillery registered its targets and fourteen observation balloons were placed in position, ready to report on the fall of the shells. Tunnels were dug under no man's land in which were placed explosive charges, to be detonated beneath the German lines at the appointed time.

The Germans were well aware that an attack was imminent, but they could not know exactly where it would fall, or when. Early in the summer, the cancellation of the Whitsun Bank Holiday in England to keep factories in full production, protested by the unions and widely reported in the newspapers, gave a clue that it would be soon. The digging of new forward positions in front of Gommecourt suggested it would come in the north. When, on 24 June, the artillery bombardment began, it was certain there were only a few days left.

The task of the artillery was twofold; to destroy the German trenches and to cut the barbed wire in front of them. For all the effort made, heavy guns were still too few, and half of those the British had had been loaned by the French. Moreover, the existence of the deep bunkers was not known, and even where the trenches were smashed the defending troops had a fair chance of survival. The wire-cutting was the role of the lighter guns, using shrapnel shells which exploded to scatter hundreds of steel balls. These shells could cut wire if accurately fused and fired, but if fused to explode too early they missed the wire, and if too late they were buried in the ground. Finally, many guns were worn, or became so during the bombardment, which wrecked their accuracy, and the quality of ammunition was poor; far too many shells failed to explode, and the battlefield was to be peppered with duds. The bombardment was, indeed, massive and ferocious, but its results fell far short of Rawlinson's expectations.

The assaulting infantry gathered their equipment: full packs with necessities, including rations and water, for several days' living during the coming advance; rifle, bayonet, and 220 rounds of ammunition; gas helmet; wound dressings; two hand grenades; flares; a spade and two empty sandbags made up the load – some 70 pounds in weight all up. With this handicap a man was expected to advance over broken ground and through barbed wire to attack a trench under fire. Old hands quietly ditched their packs before they moved off. Many of the attackers carried more, with additional loads of machine-gun ammunition, mortar bombs, wire pickets, signalling equipment, while those assigned to the later waves of the advance had even greater loads.

The smooth timetable was interrupted by rainstorms on 26 and 27 June, and the difficult decision was taken to delay the attack until 1 July to let the ground dry out. The infantry assault was to start at 7.30am, when it would be light enough to ensure the accuracy of the final bombardment, light enough, as well, to give defending Germans clear sight of their attackers. As daylight approached the British infantry reassembled in the forward trenches, groping their way forward in the dark and, huddled against the enemy counter-shelling, waited for the signal.

THE SOMME, 1916:

THE FIRST DAY

LA BOISSELLE

The thrust in the centre – along the Albert-Bapaume road.

Below: The white chalk spoil marks the German trenches under bombardment in the days before the attack at La Boisselle. (IWM Q23)

FROM ALBERT the road to Bapaume runs, as the Romans built it, ruler-straight to the northeast. Topping a rise before descending into the Avoca valley (25), it then starts its long, steady climb past La Boisselle (14), close on the right, to the summit of the ridge at Pozières, nearly halfway to its destination. La Boisselle itself is on a little spur which projects into the valley. It was on this front that the 34th Division was to advance.

For a whole week the shells had been falling on the German front line on the opposite hill, and two mines were ready to shatter what resistance might be left. In these circumstances Major-General E. C. Ingouville-Williams, commanding the 34th Division, was confident that his men could thrust up Mash Valley (13), to the left, and Sausage Valley (20), to the right of La Boisselle, pinching out the village in the salient that remained as a routine mopping-up operation while the advance to Pozières continued during the rest of the day.

In the front line, astride the road, was 102 (Tyneside Scottish) Brigade, with the 20th and 23rd Northumberland Fusiliers (1st and 4th Tyneside Scottish) to the left and the 21st and 23rd Northumberland Fusiliers (2nd and 3rd Tyneside Scottish) to the right, alongside 101 Brigade, with its battalions, the 10th Lincolnshire Regiment (the Grimsby Chums), the 11th Suffolk Regiment (Cambridgeshire) and the 15th and 16th Royal Scots (1st and 2nd Edinburgh), on the extreme right. In support, on the Tara-Usna (24) line a mile to the rear, was 103 (Tyneside Irish) Brigade, composed of the 24th, 25th, 26th and 27th Battalions (1st, 2nd, 3rd, and 4th Tyneside Irish), Northumberland Fusiliers.

On 1 July, at 7.28am, the mines exploded. Y Sap (13), next to the road, was charged with 46,000 pounds of ammonal, and Lochnagar (20), to the south-east of the village, with 60,000. The effect was shattering. Huge columns of earth rose into the sky and great clods of the chalky soil cascaded to earth.

The strongpoints they had been designed to destroy were put out of action, and, as the guns stilled for a moment to increase their range (so as not to bombard the advancing infantry, and to shell German reinforcements mustering in the reserve trenches behind their front line), the bagpipes of the Tyneside Scottish could be heard piping the men forward. In eight successive waves the front-line troops scrambled from their trenches, and in the straight lines prescribed, officers in front, set off at a walk to traverse the half-mile to the German trenches. Behind them on the gentle slope, the Tyneside Irish started down the open hillside.

Throughout the ferocious barrage of the previous week the Germans had hidden in their bunkers, tormented by the incessant concussions as their barbed wire entanglements and trenches were battered by artillery fire. But they survived. And so did most of the wire, untouched by the inaccurate shrapnel, rather than high-explosive, shells. The silence as the barrage lifted was the signal for them

Right: The British front line (blue dashes) and German trenches (red) at La Boisselle as corrected on 16 May 1916. German trenches are shown as crenellated where 'apparently organized for fire', and barbed wire as a row of crosses. Round dots indicate 'earthworks' and when shown with an arrow, observation points. Little red squares, indicating dug-outs, are notable by their absence. The map has been clarified by colouring areas below 100 metres of altitude in blue. Thiepval is to the north. (TM Accn 453. From OS sheet 57D N.E.)

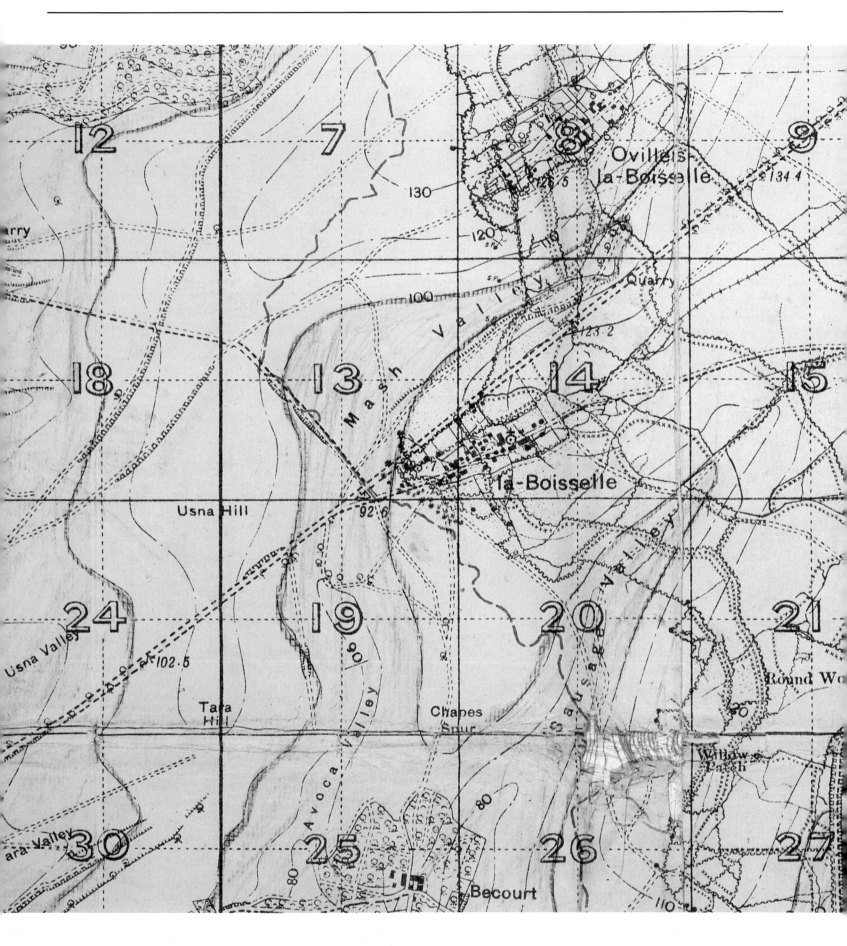

Bondage ↓

As soon as our men were in position, a series of extended lines of infantry were seen moving forward from the British trenches. The front line appeared to continue without a break from right to left. It was quickly followed by a second line, then a third and fourth. They came on at a steady, easy pace as if expecting to find nothing alive in our front trenches.

When the Germans opened fire the slaughter was immense. The machine-guns cut down the lines of advancing soldiers like hay before a scythe. Rockets soared into the sky to call down German artillery fire and shells began to explode amongst the survivors. Within minutes the neat rows of soldiers had disappeared, a fortunate few taking cover in shell holes, but most either killed or wounded. And still they came, down the hillside and out on to the valley floor. Precisely according to plan the British guns had increased their range and their shells were now falling to the rear of the enemy line on the next objective, leaving the German front-line troops free to pour their deadly fire into the ranks of the 34th Division's battalions.

Parade-ground order was now forgotten. Small groups of British survivors pressed forward in brief rushes, diving for cover in shell holes, dying as they came on. On the right, further away from the lethal spur of La Boisselle, some gained the smoking crater of Lochnagar, and still further over to the right small parties managed to penetrate the German line and capture a small redoubt some 700 yards beyond. In front of La Boisselle itself no progress was made at all; Sausage and Mash Valleys were strewn with dead and wounded.

The Tyneside Irish had set out as ordered from the Tara-Usna line, a mile to the rear of their front line, and advanced down the slope and across the valley floor, losing men all the way. On the left, before the village, they were stopped like the rest, but on the right they managed to adhere to the plan

to stand to the defence of their line. Machine-guns were hurriedly hauled out of safe-keeping and mounted, and through the smoke the Germans peered out on an astounding sight: successive waves of men plodding steadily forward, as if on parade.

La Boisselle on its spur overlooked the valley, exposing to view neat rows of the British in Mash and Sausage Valleys on each side. Far from being wiped out by the shelling, the defenders were not only alive, but their weapons were intact, and their enemies were obligingly offering perfect targets. A German soldier writing after the war recalled, with evident incredulity:

and passed through the few remnants of the initial wave and pressed on into the German lines. Some 2,500 men had set off, and now the Tyneside Irish had fewer than 50 still capable of fighting.

By the end of the day almost all of the German line was intact. The Royal Scots had managed to penetrate about half a mile on the extreme right, and the German line in front of the great Lochnagar crater was in British hands, but everywhere else the valley was carpeted with the dead and wounded, with no gain whatsoever. The 34th Division lost 6,392 men on 1 July, of whom 1,927 were killed.

BEAUMONT HAMEL

The first-day objective that took four months to achieve.

Left, above: Ten minutes before zero, the mine under Hawthorn Redoubt blows; early enough to allow the Germans to reoccupy the position. (IWM Q754)

Left: From the lip of Hawthorn crater the old British front line is open to view. The Beaumont Hamel Commonwealth War Graves Commission cemetery occupies the forward assault trench. (MFME H/S 4/32)

Below: Infantry wait to move up from a support trench for the attack on Beaumont Hamel. (IWM Q64)

THE MOST northerly sector of the main attack was at Beaumont Hamel (11), a village tucked away north of the River Ancre at the head of a little valley. To the east the land rose to a broad, fertile plateau which was then heavily fortified by the Germans with the Munich and Frankfort trench systems, while to the west the undulating country provided the Germans with excellent defensive positions along Hawthorn Ridge (10). Immediately before Beaumont Hamel itself the ridge fell steeply to a wide valley gently rising to the village of Auchonvillers (9) behind the British line. From the height of the ridge the Germans overlooked the British front-line trenches and the communication trench system, Jacob's Ladder, that served them.

Geoffrey Malins was the first man to be appointed to the new post of Official War Office Kinematographer. During the last days of June he was sent to this sector to film the preparations for attack and the action on 'The Day' itself. The weather, he reported, was vile: a nasty, drizzly mist like a bad November day in England. The roads were plastered with mud and the noise of the bombardment was incessant. Making his way forward, burdened with his cumbersome movie camera, film, and tripod, he had to take shelter in a ditch as the German shells raked the approaches to the line. Much of one afternoon was spent filming the destruction of Beaumont Hamel.

I looked out on the village, or rather the late site of it. It was absolutely flattened out, with the exception of a few remaining stumps of trees, which used to be a beautiful wood, near which the village nestled ... Our guns were simply pouring shells on the Boche. The first of the 15-inch came over and exploded with a deafening roar. The sight was stupefying ... How in the world anything could live in such a maelstrom of explosive it is difficult to conceive.

As he filmed over the next few days Malins narrowly escaped being hit on several occasions. The Germans retaliated to the Allied shelling with high-explosive and tear gas. Seconds after Malins had spilled the tea they were brewing as he dived for cover, another shell killed the two angry soldiers he had disturbed. A British trench mortar unit was blown to pieces when their ammunition store was hit, destroying part of the front line and leaving a crater 30 yards across.

As dawn broke on 1 July, Malins was roused from his chilly berth in a dug-out to film the men in the Sunken Road, a position created by tunnelling from the front line to reach a jumping-off point closer to the German lines. The enemy shelling was

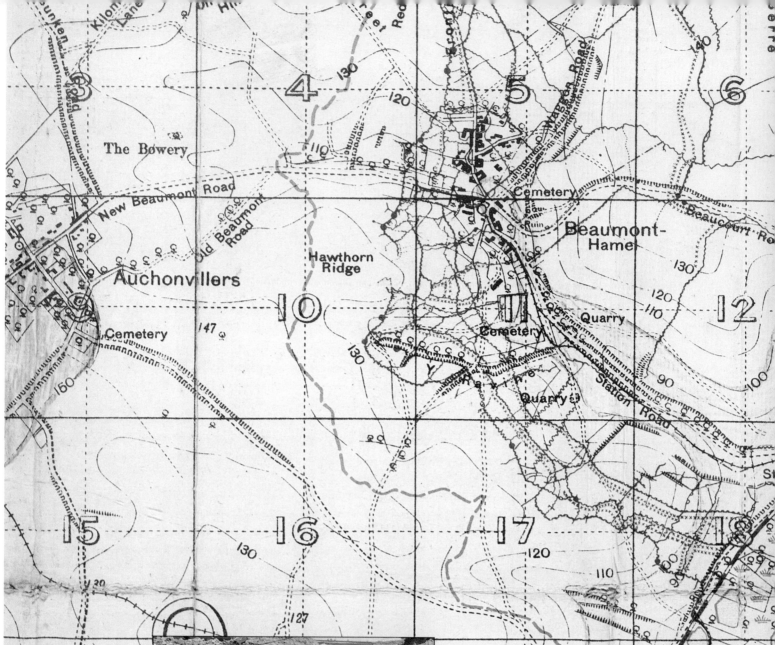

more intense than ever, and the way was clogged with wounded coming back and munitions being taken forward. He squeezed through the tunnel, scarcely wide enough for two men to pass and too low to stand upright, to find the 1st Lancashire Fusiliers crouching in what cover the road provided and ready to advance. After filming them, he hurried back to find his vantage point from which to film the firing of the mine beneath the Hawthorn Redoubt, and the attack itself.

Bidding my man collect the tripod and camera, I made for the position on Jacob's Ladder . . . a "whizz-bang" fell and struck the parapet . . . the position was absolutely no use now. I hastily fixed my camera on the side of a small bank, this side of our firing trench, with my lens pointing towards the Hawthorn Redoubt . . .

Time: 7.19 a.m . . . I started turning the handle, two revolutions per second, no more, no less . . . Surely it was time. It seemed to me I had been turning for hours. I looked at the exposure dial. I had used over a thousand feet . . . my film might run out before the mine blew.

Then it happened.

The ground where I stood gave a mighty convulsion. It rocked and swayed. I gripped hold of my tripod to steady myself. Then for all the world like a gigantic sponge, the earth rose in the air to the height of hundreds of feet. Higher and higher it rose, and with a horrible grinding roar the earth fell back upon itself, leaving in its place a mountain of smoke.

I swung my camera round on to our own parapets.

Bottom: The time-softened trenches of the British front line in the Newfoundland Memorial Park above Y Ravine at Beaumont Hamel. (MFME H/S 4/19)

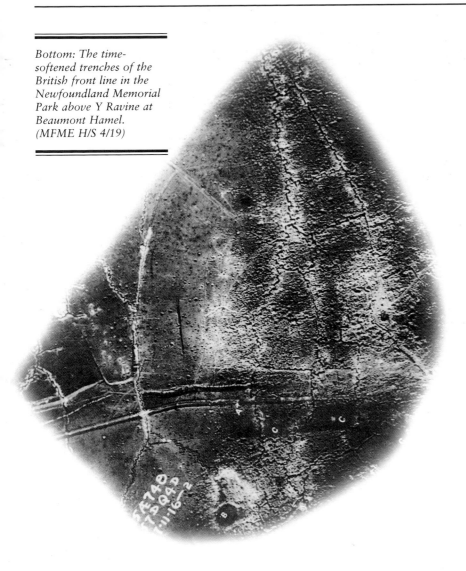

Left: An aerial photograph of the battlefield of Beaumont Hamel made in November 1916, after the village had been taken by the British. Hawthorn crater, bottom, is marked 'B', while 'A' indicates a tank abandoned on the road just in front of the German lines below and right and 'C' the shadow thrown by a steep bank. The British lines are on the left with the question-mark of Jacob's Ladder curving down to the main forward trench. The sunlight from the south-west lights up the opposite side of shell-holes, giving them the appearance of water droplets. (TM 5086/E2)

fire. He asked an officer how things were going.

'God knows . . . Everything is so mixed up. The General said this was the hardest part of the line to get through, and my word it seems like it, to look at our poor lads.'

I could see them strewn all over the ground, swept down by the accursed machine-gun fire.

The reserves were thrown in, the 1st Essex Regiment and the 1st Battalion, the Royal Newfoundland Regiment. The island off the Canadian coast had raised a regiment in support of the motherland, and this was their first action. Their attack at Beaumont Hamel, south of what was by now Hawthorn Crater, against a salient around Y Ravine (10-11), lasted half an hour. Of the 752 men who advanced over that ground, only 68 emerged unscathed. They started from support trenches, half a mile back from the British front line, and had to pass through the gaps in their own barbed wire. Where they bunched up, the German machine-gun fire cut them down. Still the survivors pushed forward, even up to the German lines themselves, where the last few fell. The land on which they gave so much is now a memorial park, still criss-crossed with trenches.

Malins filmed on. The walking wounded staggered back, shocked and numb. The cameraman witnessed the roll-call of one of the units.

In one little space there were just two thin lines – all that was left of a glorious regiment (barely one hundred men) . . . The sergeant stood there with notebook resting on the end of his rifle, repeatedly putting his pencil through names that were missing.

By the end of the day the gains were heart-breakingly small. A handful of men had managed to reach the edge of Hawthorn Crater, but the Germans had been given time to seize the opposite side and the position could not be held. It would be more than four months before a further advance could be achieved in this sector.

The engineers were swarming over the top, and streaming along the sky-line . . . Then another signal rang out, and from the trenches in front of me, our wonderful troops went over the top. What a picture it was! They went over as one man. I could see while I was exposing, that numbers were shot down before they reached the top of the parapet; others just the other side.

Because the smoke obscured the scene, Malins was unable to see the progress of the fight. Perhaps just as well, for here, as at La Boisselle, the artillery had not destroyed the German defenders and the deadly hail of machine-gun fire and the rain of shells from the German guns prevented almost all the attackers even from reaching the German wire, let alone from taking the trenches. As the fire slackened, Malins peered forward. The British shells were now falling beyond the village, leaving the German forward positions unhampered in laying down their

THIEPVAL

*A memorial to the missing, and
an enduring symbol of sacrifice.*

Between Beaumont Hamel, at the northern end of the attacking front, and La Boisselle in the centre, the British front line was established where the French had arrived in September 1914 to halt the German advance. Clothing the western slope down to the river, Thiepval Wood (30) offered some shelter and the front line ran along its eastern edge. To the north the river curves away eastwards around St Pierre Divion and to the south, below the German fortification known as the Leipzig Redoubt (31), a shallow valley cuts into the higher ground north of Ovillers towards Mouquet Farm, beyond the Pozières-Thiepval road. Mouquet Farm itself had been converted by the Germans into a fortress, and between Thiepval and St Pierre Divion a huge fortification had been built, the Schwaben Redoubt (19), together with the complex of trenches that characterized the whole of the German front line.

Immediately in front of Thiepval, where the château (25) then stood and where now the massive memorial to the missing of the Somme dominates the skyline, the 15th Lancashire Fusiliers (1st Salford Pals) and the 16th Northumberland Fusiliers (Newcastle Commercials) launched the initial assault. Not a man of the six waves of troops even reached the German wire. The final waves were wisely held back from futile sacrifice and, manning their trenches once more, laid down fire on the enemy. To the south, from Campbell Avenue, men of the 32nd Division had worked their way forward before the bombardment lifted and then rushed the Leipzig Redoubt, taking part of the position. Attempts to reinforce them were prevented by machine-gun fire and, in a rare instance of flexibility in the use of the artillery, two howitzers were detailed to support the consolidation of the gains.

In the wood the men of the 36th (Ulster) Division were in fine fighting spirits. 1 July is, by the old calendar, the anniversary of the Battle of the Boyne and the Orangemen took that for an excellent omen. Before zero hour they crept forward towards the

German lines and when the bugle sounded all recollection of orders to advance in line was forgotten. As the barrage was raised they rushed forward, and before the Germans could emerge from their shelters the Ulstermen had swept into the first line of trenches. From there they pressed forward once more into the Schwaben Redoubt itself. Here resistance was tough, for the defenders had not been caught in their dug-outs. Meanwhile the Germans at Thiepval, no longer faced with frontal attack, were able to turn their guns on the flank of the Ulsters, and as the next wave, the four Belfast battalions of 107 Brigade, came through they found themselves under heavy enfilading fire. Major George Gaffikin of the 9th Royal Irish Rifles (West Belfast) waved his orange sash and cried 'Come on, boys! No surrender!' and the men hurled themselves forward.

The fight for the Schwaben Redoubt was long

Right: The British front line (blue dashes) and the German trenches (red) at Thiepval as at 16 May 1916. Station Road (18) leads to Beaumont Hamel and the road out of Thiepval (26-32) to Mouquet Farm and then to Pozières. Grandcourt is off the edge of this detail, top right. (TM Accn 453. From OS sheet 57D N.E.)

and vicious. Whole packs of grenades were hurled down dug-outs to explode amongst the defenders. The attackers posted grenades down the stove-pipes that projected from the shelters into the living quarters. Captain Eric Bell of the 9th Royal Inniskilling Fusiliers (Tyrone Volunteers), a trench-mortar officer, actually resorted to throwing his mortar bombs at the enemy. He died leading an ad-hoc formation of infantry in attack later in the day, and was posthumously awarded the Victoria Cross. By mid-morning the position was taken and some 500 prisoners were in British hands. The attacking troops were now leaderless and out of touch with their divisional command, however. A brief foray towards Thiepval found an unmanned trench which might have enabled them to attack that position from the rear, but they lacked orders, and had no officers left to take the initiative.

What 107 Brigade had been ordered to do, and what they had expected to be doing had they not become embroiled in the fight for the Schwaben Redoubt, was to take the second line that ran south from Grandcourt, with Feste Staufen, which the British called Stuff Redoubt, lying on the line of advance through the Schwaben Redoubt. They pressed on, but fatally ahead of schedule, for there was no way by which the artillery could be made aware of their progress. Felix Kircher of the German 26th Field Artillery was there to see them.

At 9 o'clock, I was down in a dug-out in the Feste Staufen when someone shouted down to me in an amazed voice 'the Tommies are here.' I rushed up and there, just outside the barbed wire, were ten or twenty English soldiers with flat steel helmets. We had no rifle, no revolver, no grenades … we were purely artillery observers. We would have had to surrender but, then, the English artillery began to fire at our trench; but a great deal of the shells were too short and hit the English infantrymen and they began to fall back.

There were no fighting troops to resist 107 Brigade, but their own artillery fire stopped their attack. The few who remained could see German troops gathering in Grandcourt ready to counter-attack, and made their way back to their comrades. There, in the newly captured strongpoint, the Ulsters found themselves isolated. The attacks on each flank – by 29th Division on the left and 32nd Division on the right – had failed and thèse men, who had been the only troops to penetrate to the second German line, had no support against the gathering strength of the enemy.

As the counter-attacks started the reserves, men of the 49th (West Riding) Division, were sent to relieve the Ulsters. Thiepval, however, remained in German hands and any attempt to cross no man's land from Thiepval Wood was doomed. Private J.

Above: The memorial at Thiepval, commemorates the joint action of the French and the British and also carries the names of over 73,000 British and South Africans with no known grave who died in the fighting between July 1916 and 20 March 1918. The crosses of the French and headstones of the British symbolize the shared suffering of the two countries. (MFME H/S 4/14)

Top: By September 1916 the château of Thiepval had been reduced to the heap of bricks in the centre of this picture and the surrounding gardens and trees to a wasteland. (IWM Q1439)

Wilson of the 1/6th West Yorkshires describes the experience.

We went forward in single file, through a gap in what had once been a hedge; only one man could get through at a time. The Germans had a machine-gun trained on the gap and when my turn came I paused. The machine-gun stopped and, thinking his belt had run out, or he had jammed, I moved through, but what I saw when I got to the other side shook me to pieces. There was a trench running parallel with the hedge which was full to the top with the men who had gone before me. They were all either dead or dying.

The German attacks on the Schwaben Redoubt were unremitting. As each was driven off, the casualties mounted and the ammunition grew less. By the evening the Ulsters were forced to retire to the old German front line, where they were at last relieved by the West Yorkshires. The adversaries were to occupy these same positions for the next three months. The Ulsters had lost some 2,000 dead and 2,700 wounded; 165 were taken prisoner.

Like so many of the regiments of the New Army, those making up the Ulster Division consisted of numerous groups of men who had enlisted in the same unit; neighbours and brothers fought side by side. From the little town of Bushmills, close by the Giant's Causeway, many of the men joined the 12th Battalion, Royal Irish Rifles (Central Antrim), and another Bushmills man, Second Lieutenant Sir Edward MacNaughten, Bart, was seconded to the battalion from the Black Watch. On 1 July they were on the left flank of the Ulster line, on the left of the River Ancre. Twenty-three men from Bushmills died that day, of whom only six have known graves. Alex Craig was twenty-seven. His younger brother, Samuel, was twenty. John McGowan was nineteen, his brother James eighteen; both died, one helping the other. MacNaughten, who was twenty, was killed. Bushmills, with a population not much in excess of 2,500, lost nearly a quarter of all its men killed in the First World War on this one day. Private Robert Quigg won the Victoria Cross on 1 July, for going out under fire seven times to rescue wounded men, until forced to stop by exhaustion. The other decorations won by Bushmills men by 1918 would number two Military Crosses, seven Military Medals, two Distinguished Conduct Medals and one Croix de Guerre.

On 2 July the 36th (Ulster) Division was pulled out of the battle, relieved by 49th (West Riding) Division. The Ulsters had suffered more than 5,500 casualties, and the Province went into mourning. Throughout Britain, towns and villages suffered similarly. Whole village football teams were gone; all the children from a school class were dead or wounded. The impact on the country was enormous.

THE FLANKS

The costly diversion and the missed opportunity.

Above: From a position near Carnoy an 8-inch Mark V howitzer prepares to support the attack at Mametz. (IWM Q104)

Aт GOMMECOURT the Third Army had been entrusted with a diversionary attack a mile north of the Fourth Army's left flank. The plan was to convince the enemy that the main assault would take place here, and the Germans did indeed reinforce their line accordingly. The British troops, except, of course, for their commanders, also thought they were part of the main attack. Here the village (4), then held by the Germans, sits on the north-eastern end of an hour-glass shaped ridge with the British front line running across the narrowest part at right angles. Lieutenant-General Sir Thomas Snow, commanding VII Corps, was left by Allenby

to make the detailed plans. Given the allowance of two divisions and no reserves, Snow decided that they should attack the flanks of the German position with a view to cutting off the village before taking it. The 46th (North Midland) Division would take the northern side (28) and the 56th (1/1st London) Division the southern flank. Once again the preliminary bombardment would, it was believed, reduce the enemy positions to rubble before the attack. Once again it did not.

In 1918 John Masefield, who was to become Poet Laureate in 1930, wrote of the German defences:

The position is immensely strong in itself, with a perfect glacis [protective slope] and field of fire. Every invention of modern defensive war helped to make it stronger. In front of it was the usual system of barbed wire, stretched on iron supports, over a width of fifty yards. Behind the wire was the system of the First Enemy Main Line . . . a great and deep trench of immense strength. It is from twelve to fifteen feet deep, very strongly revetted with timberings and stout wicker-work. At intervals it is strengthened with small forts or sentry-boxes of concrete, built into the parapet. Great and deep dug-outs lie below it . . . Though the wire was formidable and the trench immense, the real defences of the position were artillery and machine-guns.

At 7.30am on 1 July, precisely the same time as further south, the troops went over the top. In the northern sector of the assault, the North Midland Division suffered problems almost immediately. A smoke screen confused the British as much as the enemy and the men milled about trying to get their bearings as the Germans opened fire. Most of the attackers were cut down before they reached the German lines, but the 1/5th and 1/7th Sherwood Foresters managed to get into the German lines and held out until, by mid-afternoon, they had been all but overcome, stiffening German resistance having prevented the support battalion from reaching them. A few survivors made their way back.

To the south the London Division fared rather better. Lieutenant Edward Liveing was in command of No. 5 Platoon in the 1/12th Battalion, London Regiment (The Rangers). He found it hard to wait for the signal to advance; he wanted to be able to forget the intolerable noise of the bombardment, escape from the confines of the trench, and walk upright in no man's land, feeling that if he never made it to the enemy trenches, his fate would at least have been decided for better or worse. As the time approached, he gave the order to fix bayonets.

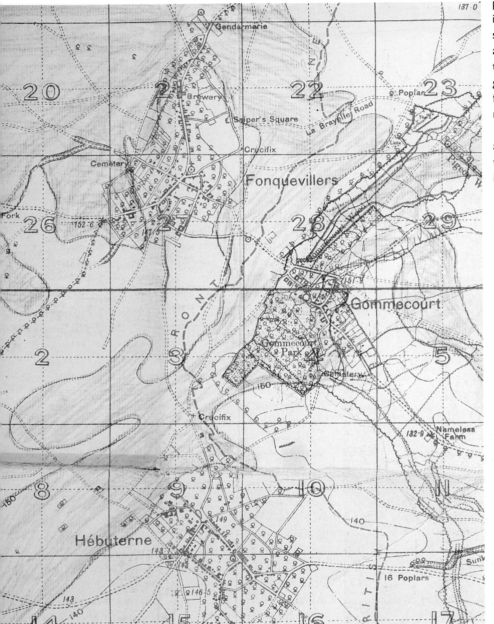

Above: The British front line (blue dashes) and German trenches (red) at Gommecourt as at 16 May 1916. Land over 150 metres has been coloured brown. (TM Accn 453. From OS sheet 57D N.E.)

parapet of our trench for that one second is almost indescribable. Just in front the ground was pitted by shell-holes. More holes opened suddenly every now and then. Here and there a few bodies lay about. Farther away . . . lay more. In the smoke one could distinguish the second line advancing. One man after another fell down in a seemingly natural manner, and the wave melted away . . .

One thing I remember very well about this time, and that was when a hare jumped up and rushed towards and past me through the dry, yellowish grass, its eyes bulging with fear.

The London men reached the German front line and entered it. Here Liveing was wounded in the leg and back, but managed to regain his own lines, though his platoon observer, Rifleman Dennison, died while helping him to safety. The Rangers had gone into action approximately 850 strong, including 23 officers. Eight officers were killed that day and nine wounded. Of the other ranks at least 142 were killed, and the regimental history records the battalion's total casualties on 1 July as 567.

The London Division penetrated the defences almost to the Kern Redoubt itself, but the North Midland men were repulsed and by the time night fell even the successful attackers, lacking support, and with their left flank in the air, had to withdraw, in the process suffering heavy casualties as they crossed no man's land.

THE MISSED OPPORTUNITY – THE SOUTH

To some extent the attempt to persuade the Germans that the attack would be in the north was successful. When, at 7.27 am on 1 July, the mine went up under Casino Point north of Carnoy (A13) on the German front line between Mametz (F5) and Montauban (S27), surprise was achieved and the French and English advanced together. On the left of the French 39th Division was the British 30th, with the 17th, 18th and 20th King's (Liverpool Regiment) (1st, 2nd and 4th Liverpool Pals) and the 19th Manchesters (4th Manchester Pals) in the front line and, with more of the Manchester Pals, four Regular battalions (2nd Bedfordshire, 2nd Green Howards, 2nd Royal Scots Fusiliers, and 2nd Wiltshires) in support.

The first trenches were swiftly overcome. On the right a machine-gun in front of Montauban opened up causing heavy casualties amongst the Manchester Pals, but was eventually silenced by a Manchester Lewis gunner. As the British entered the ruins of

I passed along the word to 'Fix swords.' [Rifle regiments refer to bayonets as 'swords'.]

It was just past 7.30am. The third wave, of which my platoon formed a part, was due to start at 7.30 plus 45 seconds . . . The corporal got up, so I realised that the second wave was assembling on the top to go over. The ladders had been smashed or used as stretchers long ago. Scrambling out of a battered part of the trench, I arrived on top, looked down my line of men, swung my rifle forward as a signal, and started off at the prearranged walk. A continuous hissing noise all around one, like a railway engine letting off steam, signified that the German machine-gunners had become aware of our advance . . .

The scene that met my eyes as I stood on the

Montauban, not long after 10.00 am, German troops could be seen in full retreat beyond the village and the artillery was brought to bear on them as they fled. At the far side of the village the British troops looked out over the wide valley and saw nothing but a few swiftly retreating grey-clad enemy. On 30th Division's left, 18th (Eastern) Division also made good, if slower, progress, eventually clearing the Germans out of the area to the west of Montauban, although pockets of resistance remained until late in the afternoon.

The going was tougher in front of Mametz, where 7th Division made its attack, on the immediate left of 18th Division. The 9th Devonshire Regiment advanced from Mansel Copse (F11) into the shallow valley just south and west of Mametz. Captain D. L. Martin, who led their attack, had studied the ground carefully, even to the extent of making a model of it while on leave. He saw that the shrine at the cemetery in Mametz was a perfect post for a machine-gun, commanding the line of their advance. As the Devons started down the slope the slaughter Martin had predicted began; he was amongst those killed. Nonetheless the 7th Division made steady, costly progress as far as the village, and by 3pm they had entered it and cleared the last of its defenders. This gave the British three miles of the German front and with the French success to their right, a six-mile

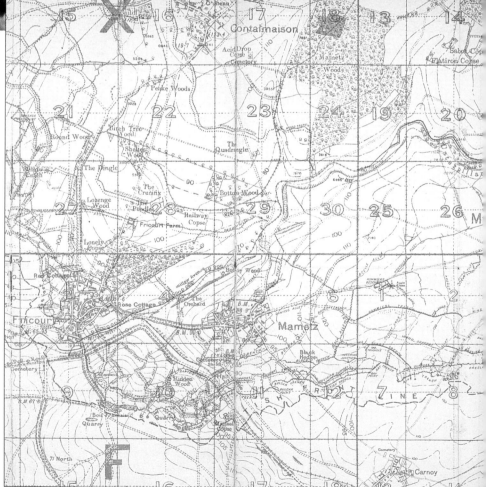

front had fallen to the Allies. To the rear Haig's be-
loved cavalry waited for the breakthrough. The
local corps commander, Lieutenant-General Walter
Congreve, VC, commanding XIII Corps, hurried to
telephone a report of the promising situation to
Rawlinson. There were at least five hours of daylight
left to him, he had sufficient reserves of infantry to
be confident his intention was prudent and the 2nd
Indian Cavalry Division was ready to move. He was
told to stand firm on the original objectives. In his
diary Rawlinson airily noted, 'There is, of course,
no hope of getting the cavalry through today.' The
cavalry were ordered to retire at 3pm, just when the
opportunity they waited for presented itself.

As darkness fell and the artillery fire subsided,
a new noise emerged from the bedlam, the cries and
groans of the hundreds of wounded lying in no
man's land. Throughout the day gallant attempts at
rescue of stricken comrades had been made, though
most ended with the rescuers themselves falling to
enemy fire. The slightest movement by a wounded
soldier drew fresh fire from the German trenches,
and the living either took shelter in shell-holes, kept
absolutely still, or died. Where the Germans no
longer felt under threat from the British, as at Gommecourt, informal truces were arranged and the
Germans themselves helped carry casualties back to
the British lines while darkness lasted. Elsewhere

any attempt to succour the wounded caused a fresh
burst of machine-gun fire. The advanced dressing
stations were overwhelmed with the wounded, and
the arrangements to move the casualties to the rear
by train proved to be entirely insufficient. Unable to
spare the time to evaluate the seriousness of the
injuries, medical staff added to the overload by
sending serious and lightly wounded back for treat-
ment at casualty clearing stations regardless.

The outcome of the day's operations was terrible beyond the power of anyone to imagine in
advance. Save only in the south, practically no
ground had been gained. Even to determine the
numbers lost was impossible at first. The roll-calls
gave figures of 8,170 killed, 35,888 wounded and
17,758 missing. As days and weeks passed stragglers
came in, men lying in shell-holes were discovered
miraculously alive, and investigations showed men
logged as missing had, in fact, been killed, while a
few had been taken prisoner. The final count was
19,240 killed or died of wounds, 35,493 wounded,
2,152 missing and 585 taken prisoner: a total of
57,470. The figures for German losses are not precisely calculable, but some 2,200 had been taken
prisoner, and approximately 6,000 killed or
wounded.

Never, before or since, has the British Army suffered like this.

THE SOMME, 1916:

TO TAKE THE RIDGE

THE SECOND DAY AND AFTER

Right: British troops on the move between La Boisselle and Contalmaison in the shelter of a sunken road. (IWM Q813)

Capturing the first day's objectives – a task that took many weeks.

Above: The memorial to the 38th (Welsh) Division at the south-eastern edge of Mametz Wood, sculpted in iron by David Pearson. (MFME H/S 3/36.)

Left: A British soldier on guard while his companions sleep in a captured German trench at Ovillers. The man on the left lies on the original, well-built firestep, while others rest on the boarded floor. The look-out peers cautiously over the freshly dug parapet created when the engineers reversed the trench and made the new firestep. (IWM Q3990)

WITH THE dawning of a new day the British leaders appeared dazed. Their plans had gone awry on a scale they could scarcely comprehend. Haig was in favour of exploiting the gains south of La Boisselle to outflank the stubborn defences to the north, but Rawlinson still made Thiepval his objective; instead of attempting to come to grips with failure, he pressed on as if the setback was negligible. In one or two places small groups of men still clung on to pitiful gains. The German front-line trench between the massive Lochnagar crater south of La Boisselle and the village itself was still in the hands of the British but they had to be reinforced if the position were not to be lost. In the afternoon of 2 July a colonel from the 19th (Western) Division joined a tiny group of the Tyneside Scottish and had their signaller, Private Tom Easton, bring his semaphore flags. Standing in front of the old German line, Easton relayed four letters of the alphabet at intervals as the officer read them out. At each signal a line of troops of the Wiltshire Regiment appeared as if from nowhere and advanced against the remaining German lines, and as they did so the torrent of machine-gun fire and shelling rose once more.

Men of the Wiltshire's 6th Battalion and the 9th Royal Welsh Fusiliers scrambled up the hillside to edge of Lochnagar crater and plunged over the rim. Those who hesitated were shot down. They managed to gain the far edge and there they held on as evening fell and fresh waves of their comrades beat against the defences of La Boisselle. By 9pm they had secured the western half of the village. At 3 am

the next morning the 10th Worcestershire Regiment were thrown into the battle, 810 men, of whom only 448 were to come out of the line. The village was a maze of fortified positions in buildings, trenches and dug-outs through which they fought as the darkness faded. During the day German counter-attacks were held off, but it was not until 5 July that La Boisselle was finally secure.

The neighbouring village of Ovillers la Boisselle, just to the north, overlooking Mash Valley, now had to be taken before any thought could be given to the first day's objective, the Pozières Ridge. The next major attack was almost trumped by an unexpected German advance from the north-east. It was not only thrown back, but on 7 July the 12th (Eastern) Division clawed their way into all three lines of the German trenches. Their losses were so great that they could not hold the advanced positions, and they had to withdraw to the second line, converting it to the British front line. It took a fortnight to seize Ovillers.

With the fall of Mametz and Montauban on 1 July, German positions at Fricourt had been left exposed to attack both from the south and from the direction of La Boisselle. The Germans abandoned the village to make their new line in front of Contalmaison, through Mametz Wood to Trônes Wood. North of Contalmaison is Pozières, on the top of the ridge. The failure to exploit the success in this sector on the first day allowed the Germans to reinforce this southern flank, with its broad, open fields and blocks of dense woodland. On 9 July the 13th Rifle Brigade moved up from La Boisselle to attack from the west with the fortified communication trenches from Contalmaison to Pozières as their objective, while the 23rd Division went for the village itself and the Welshmen of the 38th Division threw themselves against Mametz Wood.

The plan was changed at the last minute and the attack by the 13th Rifles was cancelled, together with the supporting bombardment. But the message, sent by runner, did not reach the riflemen until, at great cost, they were already amongst the German trenches. The activity was misinterpreted by the 23rd Division as German reinforcements massing for a counter-attack, and shelling was called down on the communication trenches, and on the men of the 13th Rifles in them. The slaughter was terrible.

The first attack on Mametz Wood on 7 July was a pincer operation to overcome the Prussian Guard, the 38th (Welsh) Division coming from the east and the 17th (Northern) Division from the west. It failed. Two days later the Welsh gathered once more and early the next morning mounted a frontal assault on the south of the wood. Once in amongst the trees and trenches no fewer than five battalions of the Royal Welsh Fusiliers, as well as battalions from the Welsh Regiment and the South Wales Borderers, fought a long, bloody hand-to-hand battle with the Germans. On the night of 11 July the enemy was forced to withdraw.

FORWARD TO HIGH WOOD

Mametz Wood, or the patch of torn ground and shattered trees that had once been a wood, had eventually fallen to the British, but progress was staggeringly expensive in casualties. Improved infantry tactics grew, in part, from the problems of supply; the artillery were getting short of ammunition. On 14 July, after consultation with the corps commanders by Rawlinson, an attack was mounted on a front north of Montauban between Mametz Wood and Trônes Wood. Thirteen battalions, only one of them a Regular battalion, took part. The bombardment, shortly before dawn, lasted five minutes, just long enough to send the Germans scampering for their dug-outs. The British troops, from the 7th and 21st Divisions, went over the top immediately, having moved up to within 300-500 yards of the German front line during the night. The tactics were dazzlingly successful. Bazentin le Grand and Bazentin le Petit were taken in a matter of hours, and the village of Longueval, on the edge of Delville Wood, soon after. The classic attack-at-dawn approach had worked perfectly.

With a position established at Bazentin le Petit by 9am, the British peered forward from the little ridge that overlooked the broad, shallow valley that separated them from High Wood. Nothing was to be seen except the miracle of standing crops. Clearly High Wood was unoccupied.

While shellfire and smoke obscured Longueval to their right, and on their left the advance to Pozières was stalled, here was a huge gap in the German defences. Immediate permission was asked to send the infantry reserves forward. It was denied. This was, in the view of headquarters, the long-awaited opening for the cavalry. They could move fast and might even break out beyond towards Bapaume. So the 7th Division waited. The 2nd Indian Cavalry Division had been moving forward from a position south of Albert since 8am, but had to cross ground torn to shreds by the fighting of the previous fortnight. By noon they had scarcely reached the original front line. Meanwhile the Germans were moving into High Wood. The 33rd Division were preparing to move up from Fricourt to Bazentin le Petit, and ahead of them one of their artillery's forward obser-

vation officers was cautiously working his way forward to familiarize himself with the ground. Just before 7pm he turned a corner in a communication trench to find himself facing a German soldier, whom he shot as the other tried to bring his rifle to bear. Raising himself to peer over the parapet, he saw the 20th Deccan Horse and the 7th Dragoon Guards making their long-awaited charge. He described the scene:

It was an incredible sight, an unbelievable sight, they galloped up with their lances and with pennants flying, up the slope to High Wood and straight into it. Of course they were falling all the way . . . They simply galloped on . . . horses and men dropping on the ground, with no hope against the machine-guns . . . It was an absolute rout. A magnificent sight. Tragic.

The cavalry secured a line from High Wood to Longueval, but the ground between the wood and Bazentin le Petit was unoccupied and the 33rd Division were hurriedly pushed into the gap, digging in through the night, under fire, to establish a line inside the wood from which to attack the next day. As dawn broke on 15 July, they were withdrawn to dig yet again outside the wood. Headquarters had decided on an attack towards Martinpuich to the north, neglecting all reports that the Germans were still holding at least the north-western half of High Wood (see the map on page 48, square 4).

From a point almost halfway between Martinpuich and Bazentin le Petit, protecting the former on the south-eastern flank, then curving south-east to cut through the edge of High Wood before running just south of east in front of Flers, was a powerful German line of defence, the Switch Line. The planned attack towards Martinpuich, which began at 9am, exposed the 33rd to enfilading fire from High Wood itself, making it vital to attack the western side of the wood at the same time; simultaneously, troops from 7th Division made the first of

Above, left: In the South African Museum at Delville Wood an engraved glass window commemorates the fallen. (MFME H/S 4/5)

Top: A communication trench under construction in the ruins of Delville Wood. (IWM Q4417)

Below: The Deccan Horse in Carnoy Valley on 14 July. (IWM Q824)

several doomed attempts to drive the Germans out of the wood. The situation had all the makings of disaster, and the actuality confirmed Baird's assessment. This attack was just the first to fail in the next two months. Late that night, the 7th Division troops holding part of High Wood, the 7th Dragoon Guards and Deccan Horse holding a line south-east of the wood, and the brigade from 33rd Division on the western side, were all withdrawn.

DELVILLE WOOD

Although Longueval had been taken by the 9th (Scottish) Division on 14 July, the wood that sheltered it from winter's easterly winds remained in German hands, and until it was seized no action could be taken against the Switch Line beyond. The task of taking Delville Wood was given to the 3,150 men of the South African Brigade.

(An infantry division in 1916 consisted of three infantry brigades, each of four battalions, and a Pioneer battalion, plus divisional troops such as artillery, engineers, transport, medical services, and so on. 9th (Scottish) Division on the Somme comprised two brigades of Scots battalions, and the South African Brigade.)

A ferocious artillery battle started at dawn on 15 July, and five days of vicious hand-to-hand fighting followed. A terrifying hazard was the danger of being buried alive by bursting shells. Lord Moran, who was to become Winston Churchill's physician in later years, but was then, as Charles Wilson, an officer in the Royal Army Medical Corps, gave a moving account of the panic-stricken efforts he and his companions made to rescue victims of such a fate, scrabbling with bare hands for fear of injuring the men whose muffled cries could be heard from beneath the torn earth, while themselves risking the same awful death from the continuous shelling.

For five days the South Africans attempted to carry out their orders to take the wood at all costs. The cost was immense: 758 survived, and when the brigade was relieved on 20 July, only 147 men were left in the line. The dead outnumbered the wounded by four to one. The 18th Division was sent to take over on 19 July, relieving the Scots, clearing the southern edge of the wood, and allowing the scant remnants of the South African Brigade to withdraw the following day. The wood soaked up men. On 22 July XV Corps attempted to push the Germans out. They failed. The 2nd and 5th Divisions crept forward against dogged resistance at the end of the month, but still the Germans held on, having lost nearly 9,500 men here so far.

On 13 August the 10th Durham Light Infantry took up the task. Lance-Corporal Edward Parker recalled:

At Longueval we came out into the open and found the crumpled bricks of a shattered village, still littered with bodies long dead. The village pond, once green, was now a vivid red and the corpses we stepped over were mainly those of the South Africans whose faces were blackened by three weeks of hot sunshine. At the edge of the wood we came into full view of the watchful enemy and therefore advanced by short rushes, each of which drew a long burst of machine-gun fire, and the soon to-be-dreaded point-blank stab of screaming whizz-bangs. One section remained motionless in line sprawled on the ground never to move again, and in my mind's eye one man, Allen, is kneeling still where the gunners caught him . . .

Their trenches were shallow scrapes and afforded little cover. Parker's platoon sergeant was hit in the stomach and died as the young man tried to stuff his entrails back. The next day, when bringing up the rations, they were caught again by shelling and two of their party disappeared from sight, the remainder running shuddering over ground that gave under their feet, the 'soft springy place beneath which our comrades were so freshly buried.'

Bombing patrols at night were an entirely different experience.

We walked into the front line and first visited the latrine, where a man's booted leg projecting from the bench served as a hanger for our equipment. No-man's-land in the wood was a complete surprise. After the incessant strafing of the trenches, here was a sanctuary of quiet, filled with the dense blackness of deep shell holes and uncanny shapes of tortured trees. At every step we paused, listening intently, for with so much cover, surprise would be easy.

A swelling on his foot kept Parker out of the line for a few days, and by the time he was fit again, 25 August, he was told that the last trench in Delville Wood had been cleared. He met his victorious battalion with envy at missing 'the best show yet' and was amazed to find that the booty acquired included, instead of the chlorinated water the British troops put up with, mineral water bottled for the Germans in one of the French villages nearby. The best show yet had cost the 10th Durhams 6 officers and 203 men killed or wounded.

Parker was too optimistic. Perhaps the Durhams had taken their objectives, but there were still Germans in that wood. Even after the hard fighting of the first week of September the trench on the eastern flank of Delville Wood was in enemy hands. It would take something remarkable to shift them.

THE FIGHT FOR POZIÈRES

The long, hard climb from La Boisselle to the summit of the ridge was attempted throughout July. On 21 July the Australians came to the Somme. The men of the Australian and New Zealand Army Corps, the ANZACs, had proved themselves to be outstandingly tough and courageous in the failed campaign at Gallipoli, as well as refreshingly free from the servile deference to rank that was normal in the British Army. They had already had a taste of the Western Front since coming to France. A few days earlier, on 19 July, the 5th Australian Division had floundered with incredible but unproductive courage in the mud-bath of Fromelles, west of Lille, where an ill-conceived operation intended to divert German support from the Somme, some thirty-five miles to the south, achieved none of its objectives. The well-drained countryside of Picardy was not as hopeless underfoot as the flatlands further north, but the Germans were quite as well entrenched.

At 1.30am on 23 July the 1st Australian Division went for Pozières (4) from south of the Albert–

Above: The Albert–Bapaume road, cut by a communication trench, at Pozières in September 1916. All signs of habitation or cultivation are gone. (IWM Q1086)

Centre right: Lieutenant-General F.M. Birdwood, commanding the Australian troops on the Somme, talking with some of his men at Contay, west of Albert. (IWM Q946)

Right: German trenches (red) at Pozières as at 6 July 1916. The road north-west to Thiepval passes Mouquet Farm in square 33. Square 29, top right, in which part of the village of Courcelette is shown, is in line with square M25 as shown on the Flers map, page 48. (TM Accn 8291. From OS map Area of Martinpuich, part of sheets 57D S.E. and 57C S.W.)

Bapaume road, while west of them the British 48th Division attacked from Ovillers la Boisselle up Mash Valley towards the left flank of the German positions. To the Australians' right assaults towards High Wood and the Switch Line by British 1st, 19th and 51st Divisions, and against Delville Wood and Guillemont to the east by 5th, 3rd and 30th Divisions, were also attempted, but failed. The Australians were inside Pozières within the hour and, finding that 48th Division's attack was lagging, poured over the main road to storm the Gibraltar strongpoint. Only 200 yards away was the windmill (35) that marked the summit of the ridge. By the end of the day the 17th Royal Warwickshire Regiment had managed to join the Australians to the north-west of the village, but the top of the ridge, with its two lines of massive trenches, still lay before them. The 2nd Australian Division relieved their compatriots and continued the action over the next four days before they, too, were relieved. They were no closer to the windmill, and had suffered 3,500 killed and wounded.

Geoffrey Malins went up from the chalk pit near Contalmaison Wood (10) to film the scene.

The enemy must have been putting 9-inch and 12-inch stuff in there, for they were sending up huge clouds of smoke and débris . . . From the chalk-pit to Pozières was no great distance. The ground was littered with every description of equipment, just as it had been left by the flying Huns, and dead bodies were everywhere . . . The place was desolate in the extreme. The village was absolutely non-existent. There was not a vestige of buildings remaining, with one exception, and that was a place called by the Germans 'Gibraltar', a reinforced concrete emplacement he had used for machine-guns. The few trees that had survived the terrible blasting were just stumps, no more.

After a month of battle, the first day's objective, the Pozières Ridge, was still in enemy hands. The British and Empire forces had taken 165,000 casualties, including 40,000 dead. Disquiet was at last being felt in England, where the hospitals were thronged with the wounded. General Sir William Robertson, Chief of the Imperial General Staff, wrote to Haig to tell him that 'The powers-that-be are beginning to get a little uneasy . . . [wondering] whether a loss of say 300,000 men will lead to really great results, because, if not, we ought to be content with something less than we are doing now.' Haig responded: 'In another six weeks the enemy should be hard put to find men. The maintenance of a steady offensive pressure will result eventually in his complete overthrow.' Clearly the vision of a

breakthrough had been abandoned, and equally clearly the underestimation of German strength and courage persisted.

THE HARD END OF SUMMER

The beautiful summer weather continued, sunny and warm. The flies prospered. They were everywhere, tormenting troops on the move, settling on troops in the trenches. The maggots waxed fat on the profusion of flesh scattered over the fields of Picardy. The rats thrived. The battle went on remorselessly.

The realization among senior British commanders that infantry tactics were unsuited to the challenge was slow in coming. Reliance on artillery support alone persisted, although as early as 3 August the commander of XIV Corps, Lieutenant-General the Earl of Cavan, had issued a memorandum to his divisional commanders suggesting changes. He advocated the close support of 18-pounder field guns firing shrapnel in the advance, and the immediate digging of communication trenches across no man's land during an attack to give cover for reinforcements moving up to positions taken in the assault. He further ordered that assaulting troops should be spared carrying any but absolutely necessary kit; only fifty rounds of ammunition, a half-dozen bombs (grenades), haversack, water-bottle, rifle and bayonet 'have been found to meet all requirements'. This approach was slow in gaining wider acceptance.

The Australian pressure on the German positions around the Pozières windmill continued, no doubt to the satisfaction of those who believed in steady offensive pressure. Finally, on 4 August, they prevailed. To their left the ridge stretched away, past Mouquet Farm, which still held out against the Allies, to Thiepval, still securely in German control.

On 8 August a joint action with the French was mounted on the right flank where the Germans held Guillemont and Ginchy. Just over a week earlier the

Right: On the British right flank the French maintained a similar pressure on the enemy in the open, shell-scarred countryside. From an aircraft at a height of 150 metres French troops are seen advancing under the cover of smoke. (NA, W&C643)

1st, 3rd and 4th Liverpool Pals (17th, 19th and 20th King's), the 1st, 2nd and 3rd Manchester Pals (16th, 17th and 18th Manchesters), with other battalions, had attempted to take Guillemont, which would open the way for an attack on Ginchy. Mist shrouded the fields. The Germans had crept forward to avoid the shelling, hidden from view, and resumed their positions as, at 4.45 am on 30 July, the British advanced. Still neither side could see the other, but the Germans were able to fire machine-guns at random into the fog with terrible effect; 30th Division, from which most of the attacking battalions had come, was relieved that night. The artillery had been pounding at the defences ever since. The Germans were giving at least as good as they got. The new attack, carried out mainly by one Regular and three Territorial battalions of the King's (Liverpool Regiment), fared no better than the last, this time stopped literally dead by the blanket of shell fire that enveloped no man's land. A few men got into Guillemont itself for a while, and a trivial length of enemy trench was taken, but the 1/5th King's and 1/8th King's (Liverpool Irish) had been cut to ribbons.

All up and down the line the artillery, both Allied and German, maintained an almost continuous fire. It is impossible to imagine what such bombardment was like. It wore down the gunners, and threatened body and mind of the targeted troops. Gunner George Worsley shelled Guillemont.

There were gun lines everywhere – a continuous row of them. There was no end to them – and all of them were firing almost non-stop, right round the clock . . . What really began to get to me was the sound of our own guns. The sound waves were going over your head all the time, like a tuning fork being struck on your steel helmet. A terrible sound – ping, ping, ping, ping – this terrible vibration day and night . . . You couldn't get away from it.

The French trench newspaper *La Saucisse* carried an account of what it was like being shelled.

There can be no doubt about it, this is a bombardment, a real one, one of those artillery preparations that precede attacks . . . Soon the noise becomes hellish; several batteries thundering out together. Impossible to make out anything. Shells fall without interruption. He feels his head is bursting, that his sanity is wavering. This is torture and he can see no end to it. He is suddenly afraid of being buried alive . . . What has happened to his friends? Have they gone? Are they dead? Is he the only one left alive in his hole? It's too stupid to stay there, waiting for death! Oh! To see the danger face to face! To fight back!!! To act!! The deluge continues . . . And the man remains in his hole, powerless, waiting, hoping for a miracle.

On 14 August it started to rain. A general attack on a ten-mile front was planned for 18 August, and it rained for those four intervening days. The trenches filled with water and the tortured earth became a morass in which men and horses could hardly move. In the northern sector of the attack front, on the edge of the little valley south of Thiepval, a toe-hold had been gained on the top of the

Below: The attempts to take Thiepval continued. Men of the Wiltshire Regiment press forward on 7 August. (IWM Q1142)

ridge at Leipzig Redoubt. The Australians were still in front of Mouquet Farm, but away to the south of the Albert-Bapaume road the Switch Line defied the British. They had not got beyond Delville Wood, and Guillemont had yet to be taken. Gains at all these points were the objective.

On 1 July the artillery had laid a lifting barrage; that is, when the attack went in the guns increased their range by a substantial distance to shell the second line of enemy trenches. This left the front line relatively safe for defenders to man their parapets and shoot down the attackers. Now a new technique was to be used, the creeping barrage. The guns were to increase their range by a small distance every few minutes to lay down a moving curtain of fire ahead of their advancing infantry. Precise timing and good communications were vital if the gunners were to avoid killing their comrades. A pause in the shelling was to be a signal for the start of the advance, but with German counter-shelling of stunning intensity taking place at the same time, the pause went unnoticed. Wireless communications were now being attempted, but were clumsy, unreliable, and had to be operated from immobile signalling posts. Among the advancing infantry, death by friendly fire was common.

The gains of 18 August were tiny. The position at the Leipzig Redoubt was improved by the capture of a couple of trenches to give the British a position overlooking Thiepval, and the Australians had inched forward towards Mouquet Farm, but the 7th Rifle Brigade took heavy casualties in front of High Wood, and the gains by the British at Guillemont and the French at Maurepas were trivial. Haig was, nonetheless, satisfied, particularly with the modest success near Thiepval, which had demonstrated the effectiveness of the creeping barrage.

Two weeks later, on 3 September, they tried again. The joint effort of the French and British up the valley to the right of Guillemont towards Leuze Wood (known to the British as Lousy Wood), just west of Combles, was unsupported by artillery. A German counter-attack on the south-eastern flank called for all the French firepower. The first assault was cut down, but the next attack by the 1st Duke of Cornwall's Light Infantry and 12th Gloucesters (Bristol) fared better, and by afternoon Guillemont was in British hands. Two days later, on 5 September, Leuze Wood fell at last, and four days after that battalions from 16th (Irish) Division seized Ginchy on the ridge beyond, just to the north of Guillemont. Amongst those who died there was Tom Kettle of the Royal Dublin Fusiliers, an Irish nationalist, poet and Professor of National Economics in Dublin. In a letter written the previous day he declared his wish, if he survived, to work for peace. 'I have seen war, and faced modern artillery, and know what an outrage it is against simple men.' A comrade emptied Kettle's pockets of his possessions to return them to his wife. Within seconds this kindness was set at nothing as a shell blew the man to pieces.

To the east of Ginchy, on the Morval road, the Germans had constructed a massive strongpoint, the Quadrilateral. It lay north of Leuze Wood, now in British hands, and Bouleaux Wood, just beyond which was still held by the Germans. A major effort was planned for 15 September to push north from the ruins of Delville Wood, to the edge of which the Germans clung, to take High Wood and the Switch Line at last, but the Quadrilateral position threatened the flank of the intended advance. On the night of 9/10 September the Guards Division moved up to take over Ginchy, Leuze Wood and the intervening positions, while in the centre the New Zealanders were entering the line for the first time on the Somme between Longueval and High Wood, and away to the left, near Pozières, the Canadian Corps relieved I Australian Corps.

On 13 September a message from GHQ was issued to all troops exhorting them to even greater efforts in the coming attack. It suggested a new and previously untried weapon would be deployed, and promised a situation in which 'risks may be taken with advantage which would be unwise if the circumstances were less favourable to us'.

Rumours circulated among the troops. Many had seen the huge shapes shrouded by tarpaulins and many were aware that these were not the mobile water tanks they were said to be. But what the tanks really were and what they could do was not known. Could they be the answer to this slow slaughter?

THE ILLUSION OF MOBILITY

The failed promise of an end to static warfare.

THE FIRST TANKS IN BATTLE

Left: Tanks had communication problems. Before the introduction of radio later in the war, and unless they could stop and use the infantry's telephone systems, carrier pigeons had to be used. (TM 890/E3)

Below: A 'male' Mark I tank moves forward in Chimpanzee Valley to take position for the attack of 15 September. The wire shield on top was intended to fend off grenades but it was soon abandoned. (TM 243/D6)

EARLY IN the war it had become apparent that the trench systems, protected with barbed wire, supported by pre-ranged artillery and defended by machine-guns, were close to impregnable to infantry and to cavalry. Lieutenant-Colonel (later Major-General Sir) Ernest Swinton, one of the chief proponents of the tank, and later the commander of the tank training force, summed up the requirements for a device to overcome trenches, rather than a machine to reintroduce mobile warfare. The bullet-proof vehicle had to be 'capable of destroying machine-guns, of crossing country and trenches, of breaking through entanglements and of climbing earthworks'. The inspiration was found in the many and curious machines that had been devel-

oped for agricultural use, where the track-laying vehicle had proved its ability to deal with broken ground. The first example, 'Little Willie', was built in 1915. It was high in the body, and mounted on conventional caterpillar tracks low in profile. An improved version, 'Mother', soon followed. A rhomboid profile lowered the overall height, and the tracks ran right round the rhombus, giving improved performance in trench-crossing and in dealing with embankments and shell-holes.

The vehicles were very primitive, even by the standards achieved later in the war. Weighing 28 tons, they were powered by unreliable engines of only 105 horsepower and could manage a snail-like half a mile per hour off the road, consuming a gallon of petrol per hour in the process. Their armour was light, sufficient to withstand small-arms fire but easily penetrated by shell fire. The impact of machine-gun bullets on the armour caused metal flakes to peel off, sending steel fragments, 'splash', flying around inside. Crews were issued with bizarre leather helmets with goggles and chain-mail visors for protection. Few bothered to wear these uncomfortable and restricting head-pieces, and tank veterans could be recognized by the black powdering of tiny scars on their faces. The noise and fumes inside were indescribable.

Two models of the Mark I tank were made. The 'male' was armed with two 6-pounder naval guns in sponsons (pods) fitted on each side, which allowed the weapons a limited amount of lateral and vertical movement. The 'female' had twin Vickers machine-guns. To protect it from grenades, the tank had a chicken-wire shield mounted on top – a device soon abandoned as causing more problems than it solved.

Navigation and steering were difficult. Two brakemen controlled a track apiece, and the tank towed two heavy steel wheels behind it to assist steering, while the officer in command used compass bearings and elapsed time in order to work out his position. Visibility was poor, and on more than one occasion tanks opened fire on their own troops. Radio communication between vehicles was not developed until late in the war, and the first tanks could only send messages either by stopping and using the infantry's systems, where telephone lines were intact and not cut by shell fire or the tank's tracks, or by carrier pigeon. When radio was first introduced it could be used only when the tank was stationary. In spite of all these shortcomings, however, the new weapons had a significant impact.

Haig had wanted at least 100 tanks for 1 July, and by 15 September still had only 49 at his disposal. There were doubts whether they should be used at all in such small numbers, but the cost of the

battle so far had been fearful and it was vital to find an answer to the puzzle of how to take a trench line. In the coming assault, the British artillery barrage was to leave unshelled lanes open for the tanks' advance, and the infantry were to follow close behind the armour.

On 11 September the secret weapons began their move into the line. Seventeen of them failed before they got there. Seven did not even set out. But the twenty-five that did take part in the attack on 15 September had a wonderful effect. Geoffrey Malins had been sent back from London for the occasion, though what he was to film was kept a secret.

It was 4.30 ... The trenches were full of life. Men were pouring in to take up their positions. Boche ... was evidently nervous about something, for on several occasions he sent up star-shells, in batches of six, which lighted up the whole ridge like day, and until they were down again I stood stock still ... All at once it seemed as though the sky had lightened ... 'What's that, sir?' said the man at my side ... For a moment I could discern nothing. Then, gradually out of the early morning mist a huge, dark, shapeless object evolved ...

What in the world was it? For the life of me I could not take my eyes off it. The thing – I really don't know how else to describe it – ambled forward, with slow, jerky, uncertain movements ... At one moment its nose disappeared, then with a slide and an upward glide it climbed to the other side of a deep shell crater which lay in its path ...

It waddled, it ambled, it jolted, it rolled, it – well it did everything in turn and nothing wrong ... It came to a crater. Down went its nose; a slight dip, and a clinging, crawling motion, and it came up merrily on the other side. And all the time as it slowly advanced, it

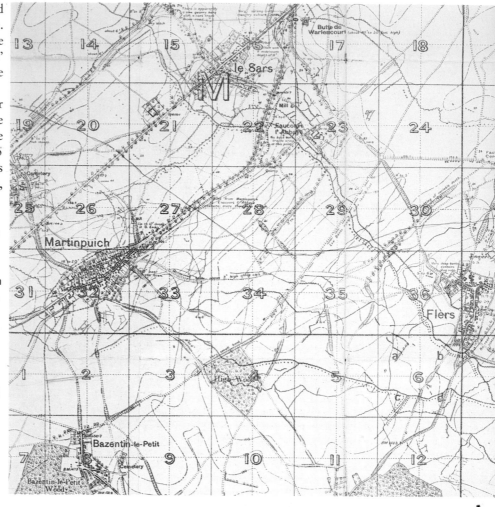

breathed and belched forth tongues of flame; its nostrils seemed to breathe death and destruction, and the Huns, terrified by its appearance, were mown down like corn falling to the reaper's sickle.

Malins was in front of Martinpuich (M32) with the 7/8th King's Own Scottish Borderers, 10th Cameronians (Scottish Rifles) and 11th Argyll and Sutherland Highlanders, battalions from two brigades (45 and 46 Brigades) of 15th (Scottish) Division. With the tank advance leading the way, they took the village. On the eastern flank, where 14th (Light) Division attacked east of Delville Wood, the only tank of three allotted to the attack to make it to the wood was D1. With bombers (grenade-throwers) from the 6th King's Own Yorkshire Light Infantry it made its way round the eastern end of the wood to attack Hop Trench and Ale Alley. Lance-Corporal Lee Lovell followed behind it.

The tank waddled on with its guns blazing and we could see Jerry popping up and down, not knowing what to do, whether to stay or run. We Bombers were sheltering behind the tank peering round and anxious to let Jerry have our bombs. But we had no need of them. The Jerries waited until our tank was only a few yards away and then fled – or hoped to! The tank just shot them down and the machine-guns, the post itself, the dead and the wounded who hadn't been able to run, just disappeared. The tank went right over them.

The trenches which had, for so long, secured the German positions on the edge of Delville Wood were gone. The tank itself then suffered a direct hit from a German shell and was destroyed. To the right

Above: German trenches (red) as at 3 September 1916 in the area of Flers-Courcelette. The outskirts of Courcelette are in square M25. Delville Wood is at the bottom, square 12. The original map is annotated 'Donor: W. Vickers, MM, RE. The line running through squares M19, 20, 27, 28, 29, 30 and N25, 32, T3, 9, 15 and 21 was marked in pencil the night after the attack and gives an idea of the ground gained and the bulge round Flers demonstrates the advantage gained by the surprise use of tanks.' (TM Accn 2458. From OS sheet 57C S.W.)

Left: A tank stuck in a shell hole could provide cover for the infantry but attracted shell fire from the enemy. The crew can be seen wearing the leather helmets intended to protect them when on the move in their cramped vehicle, but they have removed the chain-mail masks. Mark I tanks used trailing wheels to aid steering.(TM 927/E7)

things did not go so well. On 14th Division's right was the Guards Division, with 6th Division on their right attacking towards the Quadrilateral. In that attack the 9th Norfolks were strafed in their jump-off trench by a tank which lost its bearings, while 1 and 2 Guards Brigades never got the ten tanks that were meant to spearhead their attack; of the five that made it to the start line, all became unserviceable or lost direction. In the confusion the 2nd Grenadiers and the 2nd and 3rd Coldstream got separated. In spite of their vulnerability and the loss of two-thirds of their men, they managed to take the Triangle strongpoint, some 500 yards north of the Quadrilateral, before noon. On this day Raymond Asquith of the 3rd Grenadier Guards, son of Britain's Prime Minister, was mortally wounded.

North of Delville Wood, in 14th (Light) Division's sector, a single tank, D3, led the way forward, smashing through the enemy wire in textbook style. Switch Trench (2-6) was taken, and the infantry – the 8th Rifle Brigade and 8th King's Royal Rifle Corps – swept forward to the next trench line, though their supporting tank had been knocked out by then. On 14th Division's left 41st Division attacked towards Flers; on their left the troops of the New Zealand Division battalions, from their positions north-west of Delville Wood, pushed forward and captured the section of the Switch Line facing them, then pressed on and took the German positions west and north-west of Flers, and were thus able to consolidate a position on the crest of the ridge. The tank effort in High Wood (4), on the New Zealanders' left, was a failure, however, as the terrain was impassable to the new machines. But with success on either flank – for 50th Division took Hook Trench to the west of the wood – it became possible, though horribly expensive in men, for the 47th (1/2nd London) Division (made up of Territorials) to push the Germans out of their lines, and by the middle of the day High Wood was, at last, in British hands. Away to the west of 15th Division at Martinpuich, and north of the Albert–Bapaume road, the 2nd and 3rd Canadian Divisions headed for Courcelette. They outran their tank support and took the village.

The Royal Flying Corps was intensely active that day. Seventy enemy artillery batteries were attacked and nineteen German aircraft shot down. Two-seater aircraft flew patrols to spot targets and fall of shot for the artillery, and in support of the troops on the ground the British pilots machine-gunned enemy trenches and forming-up points, as well as any reinforcements they spotted heading for the hard-pressed German positions.

Between Delville Wood and High Wood the

41st Division were new in the line. They enjoyed the support of seven of the ten tanks allocated to their sector, and their enthusiasm was also so great that they beat the machines to the first line of German trenches. From there on they followed the vehicles of D Company, Heavy Machine Gun Regiment (as the Tank Corps was originally known) through the Switch Line and by noon D16 was in the main street of Flers (M36). It was seen by an observer aircraft of the RFC and the news was soon passed to head-quarters. The advance was, by the standards of this static war, remarkable, but the casualties had still been heavy and the majority of the tanks were now either stuck, destroyed or broken down. The Germans rushed reinforcements forward and the attack petered out. The hoped-for breakthrough never came and the waiting cavalry were once again sent back to their quarters.

That the day was a success is undoubted, but Winston Churchill, a prime mover in the development of the tank, complained 'My poor "land battleships" have been let off prematurely and on a petty scale.' However, it is certain that, at the state of technical development then attained, five times the number would not have done much better; they were too slow and too unreliable. What they had achieved was of immense value. Not only had they taken part in an advance of over 2,000 yards, but they had given the enemy a profound blow to morale and the British Army the invaluable gift of hope in battle conditions of unprecedented horror.

SITUATION NORMAL

Some two and a half miles to the rear, behind Mont-auban, the 10th Durham Light Infantry, one of the 14th (Light) Division's reserve battalions, were coming up into the line, eager to see this new weapon, the tank. Their brigade, 43, was to take over from 42 Brigade, now holding a line running east from the northern outskirts of Flers. Their first task was to move munitions up to Delville Wood. Mortar bombs were carried up on 14 September, six of them by each man, and the round trip took ten hours. No sooner were they back at Pommiers Redoubt, between Mametz and Montauban, than they were turned out again, this time to carry 'toffee apples', mortar shells which weighed 60 pounds. That done, the rest they expected was denied them; another journey with yet more munitions was made before they could sleep. On the afternoon of 15 September they made their way forward through Delville Wood itself, curious at suffering no casualties. Climbing to the ridge through German shell fire they took shelter

in the craters and admired the view the enemy had enjoyed of every movement in the wood they had just left. They lay under shell fire until night, when they went forward to relieve the 9th Rifle Brigade. They were surprised at the distance they had to go before they found them. In the morning they were to attack towards Gueudecourt, less than a mile north-east of Flers, as part of a general assault by II, Canadian, III, XV and XIV Corps to capitalize on the previous day's successes.

The Durhams were miners. Scornful of the Rifle Brigade's trench-making, they set to at once to make proper trenches. Lance-Corporal Parker, a southerner himself, held that the Durhams dug for pleasure. He spent the night in a forward observation post, looking out for a counter-attack, and was recalled to a deep, secure trench for breakfast. Mail was, to his surprise, being distributed and Parker got a parcel of chocolate bars. He realized he had been twenty years old for the past three days.

At dawn the 10th Durhams went over the top, at first running forward unmolested, then through heavier and yet heavier rifle and machine-gun fire. The line thinned as they went. Their forward rushes became shorter and shorter. Eventually Parker found himself on the forward slope of a small ridge above a shallow valley that rose suddenly towards the village of Gueudecourt (N26). Only one other man was in sight, and as he turned his head in response to Parker's call, blood spouted through his hair and down his features. Parker, alone, lay still, daydreaming until the firing died down, then hurled

Above: An advanced field battery makes use of a shell hole at Sunken Wood, a position taken on 15 September. (IWM Q4413)

Right: New Zealand troops consolidate the gains of the Battle of Flers-Courcelette by joining shell holes to make a trench near Martinpuich. (IWM Q193)

himself into a shell hole. To his pleasure he found one of his companions, 'poor old Stone, the deaf man,' already there. And there they stayed. They saw only one other British soldier that day, their commanding officer's runner, who told them the battalion was scuppered. Parker saw plenty of Germans.

In the afternoon a whole company of Jägers [literally, hunters, but meaning light troops roughly equivalent to British light infantry] rushed forward about one or two hundred yards to our right front. I kicked Stone and began firing rapidly over the top of the crater. By the time he had joined me, the dark green figures . . . began to falter, falling fast under our enfilading fire . . . We kept up the fire until all movement ceased and our ammunition was exhausted. When we looked at the bottom of the shell hole, there were two or three hundred empty cartridge cases under our feet . . . We began to realize that we had wiped out the whole company. It seemed strange that no one on the British side joined in. Clearly we were alone.

As evening drew near it became clear no one knew they were there. A heavy British barrage fell around them, threatening to finish them off and sending them burrowing into the sides of their crater for shelter. When darkness fell they made their way to the summit of the ridge and found two or three other survivors with whom they dug a trench and scavenged ammunition, grenades and food from the corpses that lay along the skyline. There they readied themselves for a dawn counter-attack. Footsteps alerted them. Out of the darkness emerged their CO and the adjutant, who rebuked them for being too far forward. They crept back to join a party of about forty, and dug in again. When dawn came up Parker was out in no man's land looking for wounded to bring in and had to retreat quickly to rejoin his fellows and tramp back towards Delville Wood. On reaching Pommiers Redoubt once more they found food for the 500 men of their battalion who had set out. There were fifty of them to eat it. Back at their billets in Maricourt a new captain paraded them for rifle inspection. They were severely criticized for having dirty rifles. During their four days in or near the front line they never saw a tank.

When, some time later, Parker was recommended for a commission, the CO did not know who he was; indeed, he denied ever having seen him.

Despite some small gains, the attacks on 16 September had achieved little along the whole sector of assault. For the next eight days operations were mainly confined to small local actions, night patrols, and consolidating positions won on the 15th and subsequently. Some ground was gained from the Germans, and the enemy's counter-attacks were beaten off.

WIDENING THE FRONT

The dramatic advance of 15 September, falling short though it did of the longed-for breakthrough, created a salient limited to the west by Thiepval and on the east, where the British and French armies met, by Morval and Combles. Once beyond these villages, the French had a good chance of getting to Péronne if the British could make progress on the eastern flank of this salient.

On 25 September the east was the target. Geoffrey Malins was told an attack was planned for 12 noon on the 25th, XIV Corps to push east and north-east of Guillemont against Morval and Lesboeufs; at the same time, XV Corps and III Corps, and, a day later, the Canadian Corps, were to attack in support. The day before he went over to film the build-up. That night he was with a battery of 18-pounders firing through the gloom and also experienced heavy German counter-battery shelling.

On several occasions I really thought my last minute had come. The noise was deafening, the glare and flash although beautiful was sickening. Our guns were pouring out a withering fire, and the ground quivered and shook, threatening to tumble the temporary shelter round my ears. One shell, which came very near, burst and the concussion slightly blew in the side of the shelter; it also seemed momentarily to stun me; I crouched down as close to earth as possible. I will admit that I felt a bit 'windy', my body shaking as if with ague; a horrible buzzing sensation was in my head, dizziness was coming over me.

He clambered into the open and took shelter in

an old trench, clutching his head and shaking with pain and tension, fighting to regain control. The battery officers thought him blown to bits, and, cheered at finding him still alive, offered tea.

With the coming of day, Malins looked for Guillemont. He could not see it; there was no way of telling where the fields had finished and the village had begun. It no longer existed. Shortly before the attack was to go in the British artillery opened up once more with a bombardment that even the experienced Malins found astounding. Then, accompanied by tanks, and preceded by a creeping barrage, the attack began. The fighting continued through the afternoon, and both Lesboeufs and Morval were taken. For once, the casualties were relatively light, in part because both infantry and artillery were becoming more adept at employing the revised tactics of the advance behind a creeping barrage.

The northern end of the line attacked on 1 July was just where it had been. South of Thiepval a hold had been secured on the tip of the Thiepval ridge at Leipzig Redoubt, but north from there no progress had been made in nearly three months. The dry summer had given way to a wet autumn and the weather could only be expected to worsen. It was vital to push the Germans off the ridge, to take the Schwaben Redoubt and its satellites, Stuff and Zollern Redoubts. The Battle of Thiepval Ridge began on 26 September, and involved, from the left, II Corps and the Canadian Corps, with III, XV and XIV Corps also pushing forwards from their positions at the south-eastern end of the British lines. In II Corps' sector, 18th (Eastern) Division captured Thiepval on 27 September, and 11th Division on its right had taken Mouquet Farm and occupied the Zollern Redoubt by the evening of the 26th. Away to the right in XV Corps' area 64 Brigade from 21st Division managed to enter Gird Trench in two places on the 26th, but there was 1,500 yards of solidly defended trench between them. A tank was summoned for the next morning and moved south-east along the trench, over the wire, firing as it went and followed by bombing parties. The Germans were trapped. Many were killed, and 370 of them made prisoner. British casualties in that particular part of the operation came to five. In the afternoon, after a squadron from the Cavalry Corps had reconnoitred Gueudecourt, 21st Division infantry occupied the village. By the time these operations ceased on 30 September, the British front line from Thiepval to Combles had been pushed forward, in places by more than a mile.

John Masefield came to the Somme a month later and remained until the following spring, making notes and observations for a book that he published in 1919, *The Battle of the Somme*. Masefield was commissioned 'by the Foreign Office's Department of Information to write propagandist books on Gallipoli and the Somme. The Department was frustrated. Both works were written without rancour as elegies for men suffering against a particular landscape and sketched with the poet's art.' (Denis Winter, *Haig's Command: A Reassessment*, Viking, London, 1991.) Masefield walked over this battlefield in March 1917 and wrote home about it to his wife, Constance, in one of a series of moving letters.

I was up at T[hiepval] again, & up there in the bedev-illed wreck, the weeds were certainly thrusting, so that perhaps spring will cover even that horror, the chateau, & the Tank that attacked it, & the ruin of the awful wood.

And on another occasion:

. . . Took in the Leipzig salient . . . I never saw such mud, or such a sight, in all my days. Other places are bad and full of death, but this was deep in mud as well, a kind of chaos of deep running holes & broken ground & filthy chasms, and pools & stands & marshes of iron-coloured water, & yellow snow & bedevilment. Old rags of wet uniform were everywhere, & bones & legs & feet & heads were sticking out of the ground, & in one place were all the tools of a squad just as they had laid them down; in order, & then all the squad, where they had been killed, & the skull of one of them in a pool, & , nearby, the grave of half a German, & then a German overcoat with ribs inside it, & rifles & bombs & shells literally in heaps . . . such a hell of a desolation all round as no words can describe.

Once Thiepval had fallen, the Germans had not been able to hold Mouquet Farm. It had been captured by the Canadians on 16 September, but a German counter-attack subsequently drove them out. Now battalions from 11th Division's 34 Brigade retook it, and held it. When Malins went to film it a few days later, a machine-gun officer showed him round, taking him down the dank stairs beneath the wreckage of the old farm and into the bunkers 40 and 50 feet below. The smell of rotting bodies filled the damp air; a whole gallery had been blown in together with its occupants. Off the galleries were countless rooms hollowed from the chalk, a complex like a rabbit warren. The officer showed Malins the gouged wall where the bullets from a machine-gun had zipped through the dark as the attackers broke in, and the photographer tried to imagine the scene as the fight had continued underground. When they emerged, Malins found himself 100 yards from the point at which he had entered.

Come October, and the rain fell once more; solid and continuous. What had been mud became deep mire. Masefield described it.

To call it mud would be misleading. It was not like any mud I've ever seen. It was a kind of stagnant river, too thick to flow, yet too wet to stand, & it had a kind of glisten or shine on it like reddish cheese, & it looked as solid as cheese, but it was not solid at all & you left not tracks on it, they all closed over, & you went in over your boots at every step & sometimes up to your calves. Down below it there was a solid footing, & as you went slopping along the army went slopping along by your side, & splashed you from head to foot.

Left: Pack mules carried shells for the field artillery where wheeled transport would bog down. (IWM Q4438)

Below: An ambulance north-east of Guillemont after the rain. (IWM Q4421)

That, of course, was on the roads. In the trenches the mud rose thigh-high. The shell holes filled to make deadly pools. Every movement became an effort. As October wore on the cold weather arrived and the surface of the mud froze. The fighting continued. The capture of Thiepval Ridge had been completed on 30 October, and from 1-18 October and 1 October-11 November the British forces fought a series of actions known respectively as the Battle of Transloy Ridge and the Battle of Ancre Heights. Between 1 and 3 October 47th (1/2nd London) Division captured Eaucourt l'Abbaye, and on 7 October 23rd Division took Le Sars on the Albert-Bapaume road. On the 9th the 10th Cheshire Regiment (25th Division) stormed Stuff Redoubt, and held it against two German counter-attacks. The Schwaben Redoubt, a part of which had been occupied by the British since the attacks against the Thiepval Ridge, fell to an assault by the 4/5th Black Watch and 1/1st Cambridgeshire Regiment, assisted by the 17th King's Royal Rifle Corps (British Empire League), from II Corps' 39th Division. The generals wondered how much more could or should be achieved before winter. Rawlinson, the Fourth Army Commander, wrote:

The bad weather which has forced us to slow down has given the Boche a breather. His artillery is better organised, and his infantry is fighting with greater tenacity, but deserters continue to come in; and, the more we bombard, the more prisoners and deserters we shall get. I should like therefore to be more or less aggressive all the winter, but we must not take the edge off next year.

The events of the winter would surprise him. The events of November were already in hand.

THE BATTLE OF THE ANCRE

In April 1917 John Masefield walked over the high ground to the east of Serre, between Beaucourt sur Ancre and Hébuterne, where 31st Division from Allenby's Third Army had been cut to pieces during the northern diversionary attack on 1 July. Looking west, he could see how well the Germans were placed to repel the British attacks of the previous July and November.

I stood on the crest, where the enemy had an observation post, just in front of his invisible battery positions. With even my glass I could see about a mile of English front line (as it was in July) with its communication trenches, & parts of the villages behind them. No wonder our poor men had no chance there. A man with a telescope could have sat in a chair there, & no doubt did, watching our men massing for the attack, &

at the critical moment he had only to sing out, & about a mile of batteries could plaster any point he chose. Just those places visible from that point . . . were those where our losses were worst.

At the start of November 1916 the British lines were still in the same place, and the Germans still faced them both from the hillsides north of the Ancre and from the hills to the south, where they still held Beaucourt and Grandcourt, and, on the lower ground, Beaumont Hamel to the west and St Pierre Divion to the south. The time had come for the British to straighten up their line by taking these villages and removing the salient. The rainy weather of the first week of the month gave way to dry, bright, crisp late autumn days, and the ground started to dry out to some extent. Haig had given General Gough, whose Fifth (formerly Reserve) Army now manned this sector, discretion to cancel the attack if conditions became unfavourable, but there was no need to do so.

The Germans had re-entrenched since the summer. The Hawthorn Redoubt, blown up with a mine on 1 July, had been rebuilt, and the British had tunnelled under it once again to repeat the destruction when the attack went in. Masefield states his belief that the Germans were expecting the attack; other commentators hold that they had settled down to over-winter here, and had no idea that the British intended to continue the fight.

In front of Serre the 3rd Division was in readiness, with XIII Corps' 31st Division on its left and 2nd Division on its right. The 51st (Highland) Division faced Beaumont-Hamel and the 63rd (Royal Naval) Division were a little over a mile to the south, at Hamel. (2nd, 3rd, 51st and 63rd Divisions made up V Corps.) The Royal Naval Division had been formed from men excess to the requirements of the seaborne force and caused the dyed-in-the-wool Army commanders a good deal of grief by persisting in naval attitudes to rank and discipline (although one of its three brigades was made up entirely of Army battalions, and its Pioneer battalion was also Army). The fact that they were an excellent fighting force in spite of their lack of spit and polish possibly made matters worse in senior soldiers' eyes. Attached to them for the attack were the 13th Rifle Brigade, so that the division at the time actually consisted of six Royal Navy, two Royal Marine, and six Army battalions.

The morning of 13 November was foggy and the attack went in while it was still dark. At Serre the valley was heavy with mud. Many men got stuck waist-deep and were sitting targets for the defenders. The attack by 3rd Division was a total failure, and that night 31st Division, on the extreme left,

Left: The only bit of Beaumont Hamel still standing in November was one wall of the railway station. (IWM Q4526)

Far left: British troops pick their way through the ruins of the village of Beaumont Hamel. (P)

was ordered back from the German front line north of Serre, which it had taken in the morning. At Beaumont Hamel, however, the Highlanders found the enemy front line empty; the Germans were still in their bunkers assuming that the bombardment was just the routine morning shelling. What was to become a river of prisoners started to trickle back to the cages awaiting them behind British lines. On Hawthorn Ridge and the spur that ran towards the Ancre the fog confused the attackers as much as the defenders. The Royal Naval Division's leading bat-

Above: The German second-line trench system at Beaumont Hamel, photographed on 20 October 1916. The Beaucourt road runs across from bottom left to centre right. Running north are Munich Trench, left, and Frankfort Trench, right. The letter 'A', centre, between the trenches, calls attention to the hard outline of a water-filled shell hole, while 'B', bottom right, shows the ragged appearance of a shell-hole in the chalky hillside. 'C', centre right, marks the dark spoil from a hilltop trench while 'D' indicates a dug-out as chalk has been brought up to the surface. (TM 5086/E1)

Below: The Munich/Frankfort trench system on 17 November after heavy shelling. Frankfort can hardly be seen. The crosses indicate north. (TM 5086/D5)

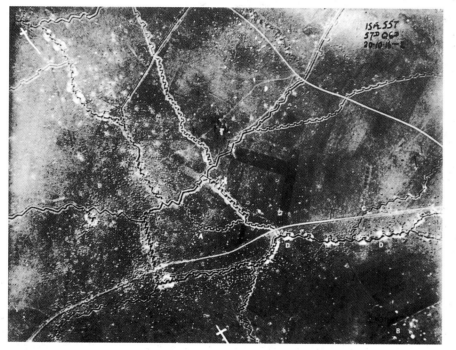

talions, Hood and Hawke, overran the German line without pausing to mop up. The defenders emerged from their shelters to open up on them from behind. The attack faltered. A twenty-six-year-old New Zealander, Lieutenant-Colonel Bernard Freyberg, pulled the scattered formation together and renewed the attack. The Royal Naval Division now held the ridge above the valley that ran down from Beaumont Hamel to the Ancre, and here hundreds of German troops were trapped. The flow of prisoners to the rear became a flood. On the Highland Division's left, 2nd Division overran Beaumont Trench and linked up with the Highlanders on the northern outskirts of Beaumont Hamel.

The Highlanders were in full control of Beaumont Hamel by mid-afternoon, and the deep dug-outs in Y Ravine were also in their hands. On the other side of the river St Pierre Divion also fell to troops from II Corps' 39th Division, who took all their objectives that day.

The dug-outs had been cleared one by one, each

yielding its crop of prisoners or corpses. On the north bank, the next day saw Beaucourt fall to the Royal Naval Division, this time its Army battalions leading the assault. Here Freyberg again distinguished himself, though at the cost of a near-fatal wound. He was awarded the Victoria Cross, having already won the DSO at Gallipoli in 1915. That day, too, I ANZAC, away to the right near Gueudecourt made a series of largely unsuccessful attacks, while other units of II Corps and V Corps attempted to drive forward from positions they had won on 13 November, with some local successes. This pressure was maintained by the two corps for the next three days.

The final British attacks began on 18 November. In II Corps' sector, 4th Canadian Division, on the right, took Desire Support Trench and several hundred prisoners. On their left, 18th (Eastern) Division captured part of Desire Support Trench and of Desire Trench; left of them, 19th (Western) Division attacked up the line of the Ancre and gained

Left: With the coming of the rains of November mud became an enemy. At Bazentin le Petit the Gordon Highlanders were issued with thigh boots. (IWM Q4474)

Below: A captured German trench howitzer is manhandled through the mud at Beaucourt sur Ancre. (IWM Q4570)

positions within 600 yards of Grandcourt. North of the river, in V Corps' area, 37th Division (which had relieved the Royal Naval Division on the 15th) pushed forward from Beaucourt and established a line north of the village. On their left, 32nd Division was charged with attacking eastwards to secure Munich and Frankfort Trenches.

Behind Beaumont Hamel, on the forward edge of the plateau that runs away to the east, these two massive German lines still threatened the newly won positions. The task of taking Frankfort and Munich Trenches was given to the 16th Highland Light Infantry (Glasgow Boys' Brigade) from 32nd Division, which had relieved 2nd Division on the night of the 14th. On 18 November the 21 officers and 650 men went forward. They succeeded in entering Munich Trench and a small party even got into Frankfort Trench beyond, but the main force was ejected from the first objective by a massive counter-attack. The forward troops were cut off by 21 November and remained so, for all attempts to fight through to get them out failed. The Germans also failed to shift them for the next four days, by which time the ninety men originally cut off had been reduced to thirty, and half of those were wounded and unable to fight. The few survivors were taken prisoner. It was the last action of the First Battle of the Somme.

BACK TO THE HINDENBURG LINE

By mid-September it had been dawning on the Germans that they were not going to hold the French and British on the Somme and the Ancre. They had already lost their forward positions at the southern end of the front, and when Thiepval fell the low-lying level ground south of the Ancre had now to be defended; the advantage of the terrain was no longer with them. Their losses at Verdun, as well, were severe, so the holding of a large salient in front of Bapaume and Péronne no longer served their purpose. What was needed was a new line to the east which could be fortified thoroughly and which was positioned where the natural characteristics of the countryside favoured defence. Then the Allies could start to wear themselves out all over again.

The cost, to the Germans, of resisting the British and French on the Somme had been immense. More than 300 counter-attacks had been mounted, and more than 500,000 casualties had been sustained, inflicting enormous losses on the experienced troops. Further fighting would reveal the loss of quality that marked the generality of the German Army in the second half of the war. Allied losses were yet greater: British and Dominions 419,654 and French 204,253. But the men of Kitchener's Army, the patriotic amateurs of 1915, were now battle-hardened professionals, and yet more men were becoming available. Furthermore, even in the grimmest and most costly actions, and the worst conditions, the morale of the British and Dominion troops had held firm, in itself a kind of victory, given that so many units were untried on 1 July.

The British spoke of the new German defences as the Hindenburg Line, a result of misinterpretation of intelligence gained from a prisoner. It was, in fact, a series of fortified lines starting in the north round Lille with the Wotan Position, which ran south towards a point west of Cambrai, where a branch snaked back up towards Arras and Vimy, and the principal Line ran south in the form of the Siegfried Line to St Quentin. This section made use of the empty channel of the unfinished Canal du Nord and the existing St Quentin Canal. The line continued with further positions north of the Aisne on the Chemin des Dames and, east of there, eventually to Metz. If the works the Allies faced in July on the Somme were daunting, these were yet more formidable. In a brilliant manoeuvre beginning on 4 February 1917, the German Army withdrew to these positions, thus, by eliminating salients, shortening their defensive line by twenty-five miles, which in turn released thirteen divisions from the front line

into reserve. By April they were established in the new positions, having denuded and devastated the area between the old and new lines.

Amongst the British the interpretation of the German withdrawal from the positions they held at the end of 1916 was, at first, quite wrong. Malins stated with complete conviction that 'the enemy is falling back, not for strategic reasons . . . but because he is forced to by the superiority of our troops and our dominating gun-power.' By April Masefield observed 'He is going to stand on the Hindenburg or Siegfried line, whichever they call it . . .' The retreat was carefully conducted, and as they went the Germans systematically laid waste to the land, destroying buildings and roads, mining bridges and other structures. The first stage of the withdrawal, in February, took the Germans back towards Bapaume and Le Transloy. Masefield observed from 'a strange place in a hole', possibly near the Switch Line, on 14 March:

I could see a marvellous panorama & . . . the Butte de Warlencourt, which is a white Butte, a very big chalk tumulus, very plainly visible . . . Bapaume was plainly visible; houses & ruins, with smoke rising from them,

Top left: The action on the Ancre yielded a fine catch of prisoners. (IWM Q4508)

Above: The Germans did not go quietly back to the Hindenburg Line. Here British cycle orderlies come under fire at Etreillers. (IWM Q2098)

Left: German field-gunners haul their piece over a trench. (TM 5040/A6)

for I fear the Boches have fired them ... Looking through a strong telescope I saw into Transloy, where a German squad was marching down a road.

The advancing British soldiers were, as usual, on the hunt for souvenirs. The spiked German helmet was a prized find, but many of those left behind were booby-trapped. A tempting jar of spirits lifted up could detonate a bomb.

The nineteen-year-old Edwin Vaughan, recently commissioned and serving with the 8th Royal Warwickshire Regiment, arrived in France in January 1917. His journal tells of a quiet, casual existence in the rear, visiting cathedrals, eating good meals, playing practical jokes. His battalion marched on Péronne on 18 March. By 11pm they were in the main street. They had seen the glow of fires in the town as they approached, and buildings in the square were burning as they sought shelter for the night. The next day the fires were still burning, and the young man saw the extent of the destruction the departing Germans had wrought. Ten days later they were on the move again, to the north-east. The scorched-earth policy was evident everywhere.

By the end of March the Germans were established behind their new lines and the British dug in facing them. There they were to stay for a year, mounting raids, shelling and being shelled, resisting the occasional German foray, and awaiting the next development.

the Canadian Memorial) the German resistance lasted all day. It was broken the next morning by the Manitoba and Calgary Battalions. The Canadians suffered some 11,000 casualties, 3,598 of them killed. The taking of Vimy Ridge was one of the most outstanding operations of the entire war.

Further south the River Scarpe runs between Arras and Douai, and to the north and south of it the British XVII Corps, part of Allenby's Third Army, attacked after the customary bombardment which blended into a creeping barrage, and supported by about forty tanks. The advance of some three and a half miles yielded a bag of more than 5,000 prisoners, but brought the British up against the next arm of the Wotan Position. The tanks bogged down in the snow and mud, and German reserves were coming up. The main action was over, but lesser, though no less lethal, actions stuttered

THE GREAT ATTACKS OF 1917

The plans for 1917 were founded on the confidence of the new Commander-in-Chief of the French Army, Robert Nivelle, that a knock-out blow could be delivered to the Germans. While the British would hold enemy reserves in the north with attacks around Arras, the French were to break through on the Chemin des Dames between Soissons and Reims, north of the valley of the River Aisne.

On 16 April the offensive began. Although the French assault dented the German positions it did not break through, and the addition of the French Fourth and Tenth Armies on 20 and 25 April to the Fifth and Sixth already engaged achieved only marginal further gains. The Germans lost 163,000 men, of whom about 29,000 were taken prisoner, but the French losses amounted to 187,000.

The British action around Arras was on two fronts. To the north the land rose along Vimy Ridge, overlooking the flat, open plains on which the battles of Loos and Neuve Chapelle had been fought earlier in the war. The German fortifications on the ridge formed the westward arm of the Wotan Position, of which the other, eastward, part was known to the British as the Drocourt-Quéant Switch Line. The Canadian Corps, part of General Sir Henry Horne's First Army, under the command of Lieutenant-General Sir Julian Byng, was to take Vimy Ridge.

At 5.30am on 9 April the Canadian attack went in, and met with considerable success. At the southern end of the line the attackers surprised the Germans while they were still in their bunkers, but at the highest point of Vimy Ridge (now crowned with

southwards along the line.

Although the diversionary attack by the British had served its function in distracting German reserves and, indeed, had made significant gains, the French troops had been asked to do the impossible on the Chemin des Dames. On 29 April a unit at Châlons sur Marne declined orders. Other units followed. This was mutiny, at least to the extent of refusing to obey further orders to attack; more worrying, however, numbers of them began to desert. On 15 May Nivelle was sacked and Pétain, taking over as Commander-in-Chief, was given the task of restoring not merely order, but spirit, to the shattered forces of France. On 27 May the growing number of desertions became outright mutiny, and Pétain acted swiftly to stop the rot: some 23,000 French soldiers were found guilty of mutiny by courts martial, and 400 were sentenced to death, of

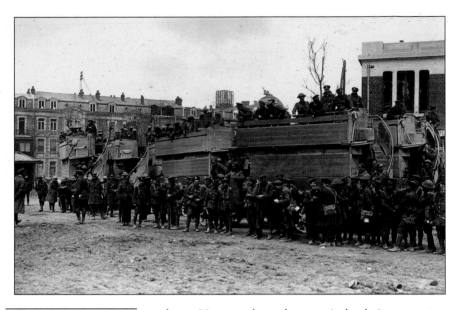

Top left: The 'Tankadrome' at Rollencourt, 20 June 1917. The tanks have been brought up on rail trucks with their sponsons removed to allow them to get through the tunnels. Fuel was moved up in 2-gallon cans; this photograph is annotated 'unloading Shell A from a lorry'. (TM 52/790)

Above: Troops embussing in Arras after taking Monchy le Preux, April 1917. The first bus to be used on the Western Front still sported the advertisements addressed to its London public; these have been boarded up and painted for war. (IWM Q6179)

Left: Mobile ovens ensured a supply of fresh bread to French troops on the Aisne. (HGG)

whom 50 were shot, the remainder being sent to penal colonies. Pétain also acted to improve his troops' lot, instituting longer periods of rest, more frequent leaves and better rations. It was clear, however, that while the French Army would defend its positions, it would not, for the time being, make any major contribution to an offensive. Any such plans would have to fall to the British and Dominion forces on the Western Front.

Haig was now faced with having to use British forces to carry the whole burden of action. Events in Russia that would lead to the Revolution and a Russian surrender were already in train, and the possibility of German divisions being switched from the Eastern Front to France and Flanders was very real. Attacks on Allied shipping by German submarines operating from their bases in Belgium were causing serious damage to supplies and morale, although, because of a number of sinkings of US ships, they also had the effect of bringing America into the war on 6 April. A major attack in the north, in Flanders, was to be undertaken.

Ypres had remained in Allied hands since 1914. On 7 June, at 3.10am, a line of huge mines was detonated beneath German positions on the Messines Ridge and the British and ANZAC troops from General Sir Herbert Plumer's Second Army advanced. One day sufficed for them to achieve their objectives, for, like Vimy Ridge, the operation had been well planned, prepared and executed. From 22 July until 10 November, in indescribably foul and muddy conditions, the long battle for Passchendaele raged. By the time the village was taken the Third Battle of Ypres had cost the British approximately 240,000 casualties, of which some 36,000 were killed; German losses were similar.

As the fighting in Flanders continued, Haig

planned a diversionary action towards Cambrai to secure the Bourlon Ridge (the feature along which the A26 autoroute now runs). General Byng, now commanding Third Army, had even more ambitious ideas; a complete encirclement of the town exploiting the speed of the cavalry and led by the tanks. Byng had 3 brigades of tanks (324 battle tanks and 100 reserves) 11 infantry and 5 cavalry divisions.

At 6am on 20 November the creeping barrage started and the tanks rolled forward. On the right the advance from Ribécourt to Marcoing was quick and by 11.30 the attackers had broken through the Hindenburg Line, but on the left the British were held up at Havrincourt until the 'male' tanks had

Right: A preserved trench and a field gun at the Caverne du Dragon on the Chemin des Dames. (MFME HS 6/27)

Far right: Pack mules near Ghelvelt on the Ypres–Menin road. (IWM Q11761)

knocked down the buildings with their 6-pounder guns. In front of the fortified village of Flesquières the armour ran into trouble. Coming over the small hill towards it exposed the tanks' vulnerable undersides to German field guns; twenty-eight tanks were hit, while the timing of the creeping barrage took the shelling steadily further away from the battle line. Supporting infantry were without covering fire. The advance stalled.

The tank losses totalled 179, but of these 71 had broken down and 43 had become stuck or had been ditched. What had been shown, despite the disappointing outcome of the Battle of Cambrai, was that, subject to mechanical reliability, the tanks were capable of overrunning the strongest positions.

THE SOMME, 1918:

VICTORY OUT OF DEFEAT

OPERATION MICHAEL

Ludendorff's last great gamble to win the war.

RUSSIA HAD ceased to be a force on the Allies' side with the Revolution in the autumn of 1917, which was followed by a general surrender. The Bolsheviks signed a peace treaty with the Germans on 3 March 1918. The number of German troops released for the Western Front was not as great as expected, however; some 1 million men were still involved in the east in pursuit of curious imperial ambitions entertained by the First Quartermaster-General, General Erich Ludendorff. His chief, Field-Marshal Paul von Hindenburg, Chief of the German General Staff, had even talked of requiring the scope in the east for the manoeuvering of his left wing in the next war. Nevertheless, the lessened pressure on that flank had already led to a build-up of German troops in the west. In November 1917 there were some 150 German divisions on the Western Front, which had risen to 180 by February 1918, and 192 by the end of March. Plans were afoot for a decisive blow against the Allies, the *Kaiserschlacht*, the Kaiser's Battle.

It was recognized that profound damage had been sustained by the German Army in 1916 and 1917. The French offensive on the Chemin des Dames, although leading to the mutiny of the French Army, had cost the Germans 163,000 casualties and the losses against the British at Arras and through the magnificent performance of the Canadians at Vimy Ridge had been heavy. Greatest of all had been the damage sustained in resisting the Allied attacks at Messines and in the long drawn-out misery of Passchendale. The majority of experienced officers and NCOs had been lost, together with a significant proportion of quality front-line troops. Further, lacking cavalry or tanks in any numbers, the infantry were to carry the whole burden of the coming offensive. New tactics were introduced to meet the situation, principally in the use of storm troops. Small units were formed, trained to penetrate and envelop Allied formations rather than rush on to them head on, and to exploit every small success.

Above, left: British soldiers blinded by gas, each with a hand on the shoulder of the man in front, shuffle into an advanced dressing station at Béthune, April 1918. (IWM Q11586)

Above, right: German prisoners of war in gas masks carry a casualty while escorted by a wounded British soldier. From a cracked glass-plate photograph. (TM 835/F5)

Left: The Kaiserschlacht was spearheaded by specially formed groups of experienced soldiers, the storm troopers. A French soldier lies dead or wounded on the right of the photograph. (P)

The other strategic arm was the artillery, now gathered in unprecedented strength on the chosen front, and retrained to support the new infantry tactics.

The choice of the front was carefully made. The temptation to strike for the Channel ports through Flanders was avoided as the weather in March was unlikely to be favourable, and the decision was taken to direct the main thrust at the place where British and French forces met – the Somme.

Having endured the demands of 1917, British forces were seriously depleted and reinforcements were not being supplied by a government, now led by David Lloyd George in place of Asquith, shaken by the losses in Picardy and in Flanders. Of the 615,000 men requested by Haig, only 100,000 were forthcoming. The resulting reorganization caused by the shortfall was destructive of both morale and effectiveness. Early in 1918, Haig therefore concentrated his strength in the north to protect the ports and secure his supply lines, relying on an agreement with Pétain on his southern flank to help should an attack threaten to divide the armies. Although the Americans had entered the war in April 1917, their first troops were only just arriving, still ill-equipped and in numbers pitifully small, though welcome all the same.

On 9 March German shelling began up and down the front, its true objective indiscernible. As well as high-explosive and shrapnel, 500,000 mustard gas and phosgene shells were fired, 1,000 tons of gas in all. The British fired 85 tons of gas against the Germans at St Quentin ten days later. Then, on the morning of 21 March, at 5.10 am, General Sir Hubert Gough was awoken by heavy shelling all

along the front of his Fifth Army from Arras to St Quentin. Similar, but diversionary, bombardments were falling on the British in Flanders and the French in Champagne, as well as at Verdun. Lacking deep dug-outs, the British front-line troops were almost wiped out. Then, at about 10am, through the fog that obscured the front, the storm troopers struck.

The British line collapsed. Not that stubborn and heroic resistance was lacking, but the survivors were too few, too scattered and without hope of reinforcement. Wisely, those who could retreated and Gough, equally wisely, approved. As the retreat developed it became clear that the Germans were not going to be able to exploit their victory, for they

could move no faster than the British. They had no tanks and no cavalry with which to exploit successes, harass the retreat, or round up their enemies, and the British had the great asset of space. To their rear there lay, first, the area laid waste by the Germans when they pulled back in 1917 and, second, the desert of the battlefield of 1916. No key assets were at risk this side of Amiens, through which passed the railway from Paris to the Channel ports.

As the Germans advanced they steadily lost more men, their best, the storm troops, and their lines of supply became longer and more vulnerable, while their supporting artillery struggled to get forward. Meanwhile, Haig was appealing to Pétain for

Above: British tanks, troops and transport falling back from La Boisselle, 25 March. (TM 889/A2)

Below: Men of the British 20th and French 22nd Divisions in hastily dug positions prepare to resist the German advance of March 1918. (P)

Below: At Bouzincourt, on the hills above the Aisne, the British hold prisoners where the advance in the northern sector was halted. (P)

the promised assistance, but the French general, fearful of a similar blow in Champagne, refused to part with troops. A conference was hastily convened in Doullens on 26 March. The President of the French Republic, Raymond Poincaré, was there in person together with his chief minister, Georges Clemenceau, and Generals Pétain and Ferdinand Foch. The British were represented by Lord Milner, Minister without Portfolio in Lloyd George's War Cabinet, who was in practice the voice of Britain in Allied deliberations at Versailles; the newly appointed Chief of the Imperial General Staff, General Sir Henry Wilson; and Haig himself. The British commander was an admirer of Foch and, with Milner's active backing, soon succeeded in persuading the meeting to appoint the Frenchman to co-ordinate the action of all the Allied armies on the Western Front, in effect, to become Supreme Allied Commander. This was confirmed on 14 April after another inter-Allied conference, when Foch was appointed General-in-Chief of the Allied Armies.

By this time the German advance had lost its impetus. At Soissons they had pushed the French back towards Paris, but were held at Noyon on 27 March. Here on the Somme they met a decisive reverse at Moreuil, only ten miles from Amiens, on 30 March. On 5 April Ludendorff called off Operation Michael, but continued offensive operations in other sectors of the front; the German assaults would not run out of steam until July. On 24 April they took Villers Bretonneux, just six miles from the outskirts of Amiens and standing on a ridge that overlooked the city, and advanced tentatively beyond with four of the thirteen A7V tanks with which they had started the day. The clumsy German vehicles rolled down the slope to the south-west of the village at about 9.30am to be met by three British Mark IV tanks, one of which was commended by Lieutenant Frank Mitchell. This was the first ever tank-versus-tank engagement.

There, some three hundred yards away, a round squat-looking monster was advancing, behind it came waves of infantry, and farther away to the left crawled two more of these armed tortoises . . . So we had met our rivals at last.

The tanks exchanged fire, and eventually Mitchell's gunner scored a perfect hit with the 6-pounder. The A7V heeled over, and the crew piled out. Seven of the new British light tanks, Medium Mark A Whippets, joined the fray and the Germans were forced back to the village. That night the Australian 15 and 13 Brigades counter-attacked. By mid-morning the Germans had been thrown back.

Main picture: British light tanks, Whippets, advance to resist the German approach near Albert, 28 March. (TM 889/A6)

Inset: An overturned German A7V tank, Elfriede, defeated at Villers Bretonneux on 24 April. (TM 883/D2)

Allied losses had been severe. The British casualties were 108,000 and, in addition, another 70,000 had been taken prisoner. The French lost 77,000 men and German losses were about 250,000, but included a disproportionate share of their finest troops. A German officer entering Albert was shocked to find his soldiers drunk in the streets, and looting when they should have been following up the British retreat. The calibre of the German Army was not what it had been. (It must be said that by the end of March there were increasing instances of looting and drunkenness among the retreating British troops.)

Ludendorff was not finished yet. Major offensives followed, in Flanders on the River Lys on 9 April and in Champagne on the Chemin des Dames on 27 May. Neither was easily halted, but halted they were; on the Marne, at Château Thierry, only with the vital intervention of the US Marines; on the Matz, north of Compiègne, by General Charles Mangin's French Tenth Army with 144 Renault light tanks, on 13 June. Could the Germans do more?

THE SECOND BATTLE OF THE SOMME

Artillery, armour, infantry and air force in harmony.

HAMEL

FORTUNATELY for the British, June and July 1918 were comparatively quiet months. Operation Michael – and the subsequent Operations Georgette, Blücher, Gneisenau, and Reims-Marneschutz – had exacted a heavy cost and the remaining forces were exhausted. Shocked by how close it had come to defeat, the British politicians agreed to reinforce the army, but only just in time. Foch held that the situation remained precarious until the end of July.

A fresh enemy, a threat to both sides, appeared in June; the 'Spanish' influenza pandemic. By May 1919 200,000 British were to die of the disease, but the Germans, deprived of food supplies by the Allied naval blockade, were weakened and lost over 400,000 civilians. The disease spread amongst the fighting forces as well: the Americans lost more men to influenza than to battle in this war.

Although the situation had stabilized, all was not entirely peaceful on the Western Front. The French conducted a series of minor actions with excellent results. On the Somme Haig now had Rawlinson in command (who reconformed Fifth Army as Fourth Army), Gough having been summarily dismissed on 28 March and recalled in undeserved disgrace. The Germans were still too

close to Amiens, but before attempting to drive them back it was necessary to adjust the line where the little village of Hamel (10) gave the enemy a position from which they could enfilade troops making an advance from Villers Bretonneux to the south-west. The task of taking it was given to the Australian Army Corps under Lieutenant-General Sir John Monash. Monash was of the opinion that the infantry should be able to advance under the maximum protection that technology could provide; not have to fight their way forward, but proceed to the objective in order to hold it. An engineer by training, he was meticulous in his staff work, and the operation at Hamel has come to be recognized as a classic.

The principal force was the 4th Australian Division, with the addition of the machine-gun battalions of the 2nd, 3rd and 5th Australian Divisions. Sixty Mark V tanks, the latest model, and six hundred artillery pieces were to be used in support. Finally, eight companies from the American forces training in the Australian sector were to be included. Each unit was allotted specific tasks. The creeping barrage was precisely defined. The preparations were complex, detailed and, at the last minute, endangered. General John J. Pershing, commanding the American Expeditionary Force in France, objected to his troops serving under anything other than American command. Monash argued strongly for their retention in the operation; they could not

Above: American officers at rifle grenade and bombing practice at the British XI Corps school. (IWM Q222)

Right: The Heavy Artillery Barrage Map for the attack on Hamel that took place on 4 July 1918. The village of Hamel can be seen between the lines marked 'Zero H A Start' and '+28 H A Halt' at the upper end of the ruled area. The Amiens-St Quentin road runs across the lower part through P25-30, to Villers Bretonneux just to the west, off this map. The line of dashes shows the approximate position of the British front line at 22 June 1918. (TM Accn 107.5. From OS map Bayonvillers, parts of sheets 62D N.W., 62D N.E., 62D S.W. and 62D S.E.)

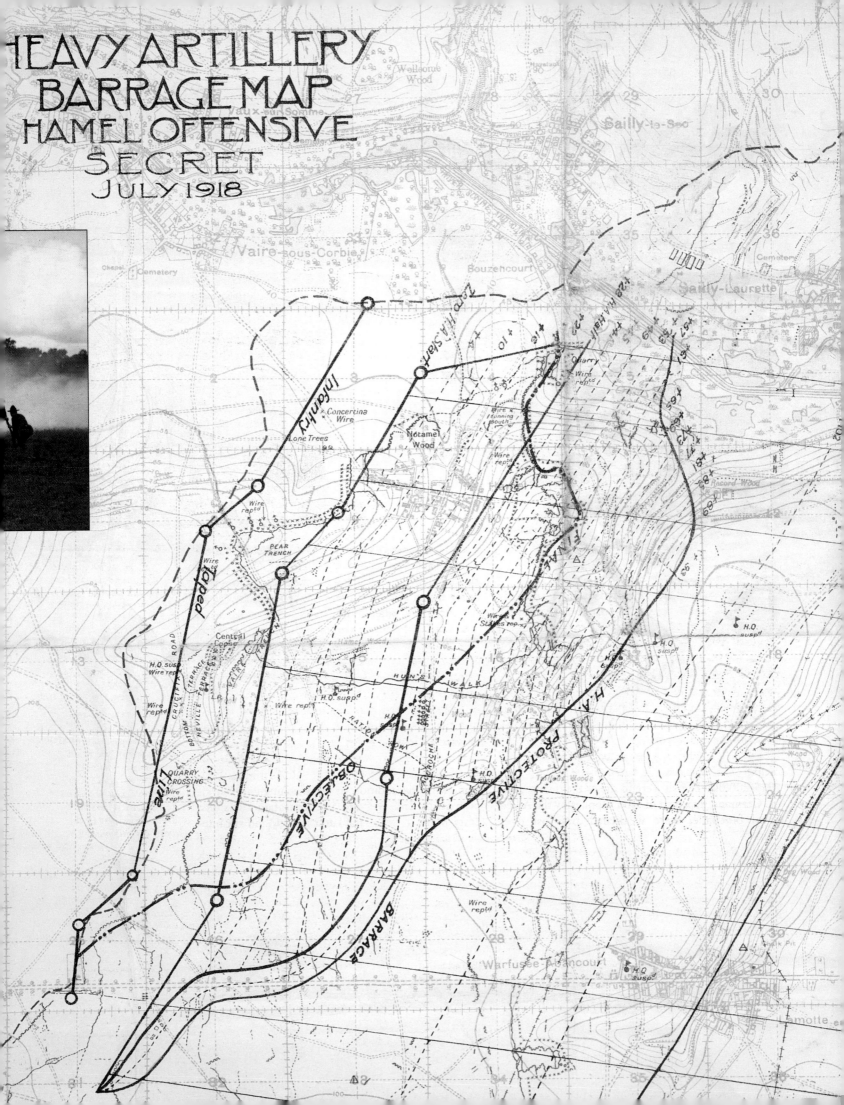

HEAVY ARTILLERY
BARRAGE MAP
HAMEL OFFENSIVE
SECRET
JULY 1918

be replaced in so complicated a plan at the last minute. The American commanders of the units involved protested at being excluded from the fight. Reluctantly, Pershing yielded.

On the auspicious date (for Americans) of 4 July the attack was mounted. The tanks advanced with the infantry close to the creeping barrage. The machine-gunners followed to secure the positions taken against counter-attack. The greed of machine-guns for ammunition made supply a problem for men advancing on foot. The problem was solved with the first air-drop of munitions in history; the Royal Air Force (formed on 1 April 1918 from the amalgamation of the Royal Flying Corps with the Royal Naval Air Service) delivered 100,000 rounds. The whole action was over in ninety-three minutes.

The Australian Corps captured 41 German officers and 1,431 other ranks, and 2 field guns, 171 machine-guns and 26 trench mortars were taken. Australian casualties numbered 775 and American 134. The British War Office published the complete battle plan as a Staff pamphlet: Hamel was a model for future combined operations.

THE BATTLE OF AMIENS

In the last fortnight of July Ludendorff attempted what was to be the last major German attack, push-ing due south out of the southern extremity of the German salient to the east and west of Reims. Their opening bombardments fell on virtually empty trenches, only a few machine-gun posts occupying the ground to lend credence to the pretence that the French were manning the forward positions. The attacks withered against the second line. The Marne salient ceased to be a threat to Paris, and now became a potential trap for the invaders. On 18 July, once again, Mangin's French Tenth Army struck the German flank, with the US 1st and 2nd Divisions at the forefront of the assault, and the British supplied four divisions to relieve the Americans, who had borne a significant share of the casualties in the sector. By the end of the first week of August the battle, codenamed Operation Reims-Marneschutz, was over. In it, the Germans had lost 168,000 men, including 29,000 prisoners, and great quantities of weapons. The defeat shook the German High Command to the core. Hopes of winning the war before the American strength became overwhelming were fading fast.

Preparations for the Allied attack on the Somme to roll the Germans back from Amiens were now complete. On the north bank of the river (P6) the British III Corps, from Rawlinson's Fourth Army, was to secure the left flank, while on the right, south of the Amiens-Roye road, the French First Army would do the same service. The four Australian divisions under Monash had the segment between the

Right: The Australian front at the Battle of Amiens, from the map of the officer commanding B Company, 2nd Tank Battalion. British trenches, of which many were captured German ones, in red and German trenches in blue at 7 July 1918. The infantry start line of 8 August is marked with red pencil from P31 to P5. The tank assembly and approach routes are shown in purple pencil. (TM Accn 4760. From OS sheet 62D S.W. and 62D S.E.)

Below: As the mechanical reliability of the tanks improved, so did the sophistication of their use. In a training exercise at Santrecourt on 12 August 1918 infantry advances behind a smoke-screen laid by a tank. (TM 929/E4)

River Somme and the Amiens-Nesle railway line (V 1–4), and the four Canadian divisions under Lieutenant-General Sir Arthur Currie, who had succeeded Byng in command of the Canadian Corps, the segment between the Australians and the French. The tanks were there in force: 324 Mark V battle tanks supported by 184 supply tanks and two battalions of Whippet light tanks would take the field. Nearly 700 heavy artillery pieces and twice that number of field guns were in place. The enemy artillery positions had been plotted by the new technique of sound ranging combined with the recon-

naissance work of the Royal Air Force. In all this preparation, however, secrecy had been preserved. The Germans were not aware of the Canadian presence and the deception had been supported by the very obvious appearance of two Canadian battalions at Ypres and a flow of false radio signals that suggested a build-up of the rest of the Canadian Corps in the Calais area. Once it was evident that the Germans had taken note of a Canadian presence in the north, the two battalions were rushed to the Somme by train.

A surprise attack by the Germans north of the

river on 6 August pushed the British III Corps back and disrupted its preparations, and the troops had to struggle to regain their ground the following day. This did not delay the the schedule for the main Allied offensive. At 4.20am on 8 August the guns opened fire. The pre-targeted German batteries were heavily shelled and the first line of the creeping bombardment lasted for a mere three minutes before lifting by a hundred yards – and as it did so, the advance began.

In the morning mist the attack went precisely according to plan. The Germans had been taken by surprise with no preliminary bombardment lasting a week (or more) to alert them to the threat. Moreover they were not in occupation of positions carefully prepared and fortified over many months, as they had been on 1 July, or as they had been in the Hindenburg Line. By 7am the Australians had taken their first objective, the ridge from Warfusée Abancourt to Cerisy Gailly (P 29–12) near the river, and by 10.30 their second objective, including the villages of Morecourt and Harbonnières, had been achieved. The Canadian start line lay further to the west, but by 11am they had come up alongside the Australians.

The tanks performed well, but their losses were considerable. More than a hundred were knocked out by enemy action and twice as many broke down or were immobilized in accidents. The German field artillery clung stubbornly to their positions and managed to inflict considerable damage. At Le Quesnel, on the Canadians' southern flank, ten tanks were reduced to a single survivor by field guns and the Canadian advance was held. On the extreme north the Australian advance slowed because the setback suffered earlier by the British III Corps left their flank exposed as they approached the limit of their advance. The British did not take their objective, the Chipilly Spur, around which the river swung, until the next day. French progress south of the river was generally slower, although that day Fourth Army inflicted 12,000 casualties on the Germans, and took 15,000 prisoners and 400 guns, for 9,000 casualties of its own.

The artillery had been on the move. For the first time not merely the Royal Field Artillery's horse-drawn medium guns, but also the heavy howitzers of the Royal Garrison Artillery, had been hauled forward, giving the attack cover for a deeper penetration. By 1.30pm the Allies had gone further than planned, having made between six and eight miles. The freedom of movement that the speed and distance of the advance permitted came as a surprise to troops habituated to trench warfare. A plan to have the light tanks and cavalry fight in tandem proved unworkable; by themselves each was able to achieve fine results.

The light tank, the Medium Mark A, known as

Below: Australian infantry mop up resistance along the Amiens–Nesle railway line, supported by a Mark V tank. (TM 64/H2)

Right: B56 at the roadside at La Motte en Santerre after the successful Australian attack at Lamotte Warfusée. The Mark V tank was fitted with an ingenious, if apparently primitive, device to get it moving if bogged down. The beam lying across the top was linked to the tank track which drew it forward under the vehicle to provide solid footing. As the tank moved forward the beam was pulled back onto the upper rail fittings, unshackled and secured for further use. (TM 1557/E1)

the Whippet, weighed 14 tons against the Mark V's 35 tons, and was said to be capable of 8.3 miles per hour on the road, outpacing the battle tank by nearly 4 miles per hour. The crew of three had four Hotchkiss machine-guns at its disposal. Lieutenant C. B. Arnold, Gunner Ribbans and Driver Carney were advancing in 'Musical Box' next to the railway line that divided the Australian from the Canadian sector when they saw two Mark Vs hit by a four-gun field battery between Warfusée and Bayonvillers. Arnold turned half-left and ran across the front of the battery, firing with two machine guns. The

return fire missed. He then did a U-turn round some trees and came at the battery from the rear. The gunners tried to run, but Arnold and Ribbans shot them down. The Australians took full advantage of the destruction of the battery. Arnold then dealt with two groups of Germans who were troubling his cavalry further down the railway line at Guillaucourt before cruising off between Bayonvillers and Harbonnières, where he strafed a crowd of Germans packing up to retire from their positions. Ribbans counted more than sixty dead and wounded. At this point in his report Arnold breaks off to suggest that,

Lieutenant m.v.Richthofen with 40 Air conquests

Main picture: A German aircraft takes off from a typical makeshift airfield, where tents serve as hangars. (P)

Inset, left: Manfred von Richthofen, known as the 'Red Baron', was the most successful pilot of the war with 80 kills. He was shot down and killed on 21 April 1918 either by an Australian anti-aircraft battery or by the Canadian pilot, Captain Roy Brown. (P)

Inset, right: No 1 Squadron RAF pose with their SE5As in July 1918. These fighters were not as manoeuvrable as the famous Sopwith Camel, but were faster and provided a solid gun platfrom for the cowl-mounted Vickers and wing-mounted Lewis guns. (P)

in future, no fuel is carried on the outside of a tank; the cans he had were being hit by enemy fire and were filling the tank with fumes. This comment made, he continues his account. Further east, at about 2pm, he opened fire on retreating transports, motor and horse-drawn, on the roads crossing the railway before turning to engage another target. Suddenly there was a loud bang and the tank burst into flames. The crew got out, on fire, but Carney was immediately shot. Arnold and Ribbans rolled on the ground to put out the flames and were surrounded by Germans. 'They were', observed Arnold, 'furious.' This was real mobile warfare.

The cavalry at last had the chance to charge. Beaucourt en Santerre was taken by the Canadian Cavalry Brigade, and the Queen's Bays almost secured Harbonnières, but had to leave it to the Australian infantry to finish the job. The 5th Dragoons captured an 11-inch railway gun and 600 prisoners, while the 15th and 19th Hussars charged 2,000 yards ahead of the cheering Canadians in Guillaucourt to seize the trenches beyond and hold them until the Whippets and infantry came up. It was 'worth all the years of waiting'.

The RAF fared less well, losing 44 aircraft and suffering 52 seriously damaged in 205 sorties flown. At the start of the day they were hampered by the mist, but later in the morning they flew valuable support actions co-ordinated with infantry attacks. As the day went on the possibility of cutting the Germans off by destroying the Somme bridges led to their being given bombing missions. They were fiercely attacked by German aircraft, including those of the late Baron von Richthofen's squadron, now commanded by one Hermann Goering. 'Richthofen's Flying Circus', as it was known because of the many bright and varied colour schemes of the aircraft, was virtually destroyed in the process. Richthofen, the highest-scoring pilot of the Great War with eighty victories, had commanded Jasta 11. He had been shot down and killed behind British lines on 21 April 1918 – though unresolved arguments as to whether he was downed by ground fire or by a Canadian airman still continue today.

Ludendorff was later to refer to 8 August as 'the black day of the German Army'. Five German divisions were broken. The Australians had taken nearly 8,000 prisoners and 173 guns, while the Canadians took over 5,000 prisoners and 161 guns. Total British and Dominion losses were about 6,500 killed or wounded. The German Official Monograph estimated their losses at about 30,000 killed, wounded or taken prisoner, and described the battle as the greatest defeat the German Army had suffered since the beginning of the war.

The Australians said 'It was a *très bon* stunt.'

RETAKING THE SOMME

To a command system used to handling large numbers of troops in a small area, the extent and speed of the advance on 8 August presented the British and Dominion forces with new problems. Communication by a web of telephone wires became impossible and radio was still at an early stage of development, dispensing with the need for wires but still depending on largely immobile radio positions. Inevitably, the advance slowed in the following days. The hope for a breakthrough could not be realized. The Tank Corps had no reserves available, and the pace of progress was limited to the speed attainable by the infantry; besides, only six Whippets in all remained in action by 12 August. The Canadians advanced another three miles and, with American help, the British took the Chipilly Spur on 9 August.

German resistance was increasing on the Canadian and Australian fronts, and Haig decided to have Byng's Third Army push forward further north, towards Bapaume. The battlefield of July 1916, still strewn with the débris of that conflict, cut with old trenches and wrapped in rusting barbed wire, offered a foul place in which to fight; Haig planned to pass to the north of the Ancre. The German Army was starting to crack; in spite of having forty-two divisions here to the Allies' thirty-two.

Between Arras and Beaumont Hamel and rolling eastwards towards the Hindenburg Line, the country was still unscarred by war, offering, it was thought, an opportunity to use the remaining tanks. For the rest of August, however, the weather was very hot and tanks, noisy, smelly and oppressive enough at the best of times, became fume-filled ovens. The Whippets' Hotchkiss guns jammed, and the crews passed out from heat, fumes, and exhaustion. The wonder weapon showed its limitations once more, and the infantry's speed again set the pace. Byng attacked on 21 August and made some progress, but not enough to satisfy Haig. Rawlinson's men retook Albert the next day. Responding to Haig's exhortation 'to act with the utmost boldness and resolution', Third and Fourth Armies resumed their assaults with renewed vigour on 23 August. The names of terrible memory appeared on the reports once more, though with fewer casualties and at far shorter intervals: Thiepval, 24 August; Mametz Wood, 25 August; Delville Wood, 27 August. On 26 August, General Horne's First Army, with the Canadian Corps attached to it once more, opened the Battle of the Scarpe, east of Arras and on Third Army's left. It became clear to Ludendorff that another retreat to the Hindenburg Line was inevitable, and that troops would have to be transferred from Flanders to stiffen resistance further south, so destroying all hopes of taking the Channel ports.

Bapaume fell to the New Zealand Division on 29 August, and the steady, bloody, rolling back of the enemy line continued. Although the prospect of losing the war was now apparent to the Germans, their will to fight and to extract the maximum cost from the Allies for every gain remained formidable. To the west of Péronne, above the marshy Somme valley, the dauntingly strong German positions on Mont St Quentin commanded the approaches to the town. The Australian division, the 2nd, facing this obstacle had become seriously depleted. Two battalions were available for the attack, but they were now at under half their usual strength. Something like 600 men had to eject a well-entrenched German force of greater numbers. Using their superiority in artillery and charging forward in the dawning light of 31 August, the Australians swarmed into the defences and harried the Germans from one strongpoint to the next. By 8am it was all over. The Australians took more prisoners than the total of their attacking force. Péronne fell, being finally cleared of the enemy on 2 September.

August was a bad month for the invaders on the French front, as well. The persistently aggressive Mangin had won new victories on the Aisne and at Noyon. September would see the first independent action by the Americans at St Mihiel, another German defeat. On the Somme front the next challenge was the Hindenburg Line.

Left: The road from Amiens to St Quentin between Belloy and Berny, where the A1 autoroute now passes, after the German retreat. (HGG)

Left, inset: From Grévillers, just west of Bapaume, on 25 August 1918, men of the New Zealand Division and a Mark V tank of the 10th Battalion prepare to move forward. (TM 883/A5)

Right: With the advance of September 1918 French civilians were at last able to return to their homes, or to what was left of them. (P)

BREAKING THE HINDENBURG LINE

The end of the trenches – and the end of the war.

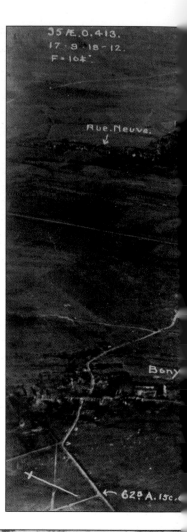

THE DEFENSIVE complex constructed by the Germans in the autumn and winter of 1916 was viewed with respect and not a little apprehension by the Allies. The Germans believed that the Allies had but small understanding of the nature of the Hindenburg Line. It was based upon the concept of defence in depth. Rather than a single trench or a series of trench lines, the area it covered was occupied by numerous redoubts and strongpoints, reinforced machine-gun emplacements, a web of trenches and carefully disposed blocks and rows of barbed wire to funnel attackers into predetermined lines of fire for the guns. The Wotan Position, the Drocourt-Quéant Switch Line, ran south from Lille to join the Siegfried Position near Cambrai. This, the strongest part of the Line, was ten miles deep and went as far south as La Fère on the River Oise. A plan of the entire layout of the Siegfried Position had been acquired by the British with the capture of a German command post on 6 August. Every last detail of the dispositions of the defences from Bellicourt to La Fère was known.

Less robust, the Wotan Position was the first to fall. The First Army, under Horne, moved against it on 2 September. The Canadian Corps smashed their way through. Ludendorff gave orders for withdrawal both on the Somme and in Flanders. All the territory gained in the spring was abandoned.

Haig realized a crucial moment had arrived. Back in London the government was still talking of the campaigns to be mounted in 1919. Here, on the front, the troops were steadily being eroded by the succession of attacks, successful though they were, and the Germans were slowly, very slowly, crumbling before them. It was vital to strain every sinew to achieve victory soon, while the tide of war was flowing in favour of the Allies. On 9 September Haig went to London to press his view that reserves in England should be regarded as reserves for the front in France. He was regarded with suspicion as a

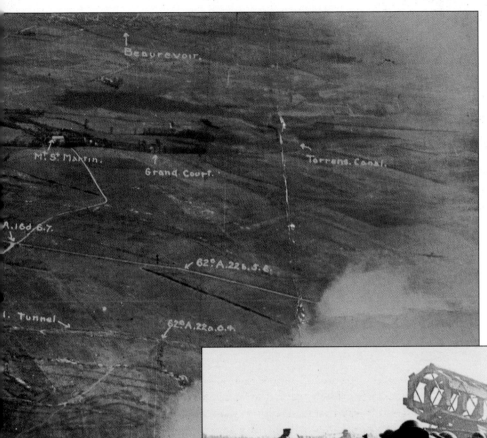

dangerous optimist, given the losses over which he had presided in the past, but coming events would support Haig's analysis, and he had at least prepared the ground for a change of attitude.

The local actions to gain positions from which the major effort could be launched continued. The village of Havrincourt, last taken during the Battle of Cambrai, fell to the British once more on 12 September, in spite of significant moves by the Germans to reinforce the defenders. Rawlinson improved his position further south with an attack on 18 September. It was necessary to conserve the tanks for the principal effort, so artillery support alone was used, without a preliminary barrage but employing concentrated targeting and a creeping barrage. The village of Epéhy was stubbornly defended and III Corps made poor progress, but the 1st and 4th Australian Divisions achieved an advance on a front four miles wide of over two and a half miles. The Australians took 4,243 prisoners, 76 guns, 300

Above: The terrain above the tunnel. An aerial photograph taken on 17 September 1918, marked with place names and map references. Bony is to the lower left and today the American Cemetery occupies the bottom left-hand corner of this picture. The line of the canal tunnel is shown and trenches can be seen between it and the village. (TM 5086/D4)

Left: The massive trenches of the Siegfried Line near Bony. (P)

Above: Troops and tanks prepare to move on the Hindenburg Line. The cylindrical objects on the tanks are crib fascines, which replaced the bundles of cut wood previously used to fill shell-holes or trenches and allow the vehicles to pass. (TM)

machine-guns and 30 trench mortars for the loss of 1,260 men killed and wounded out of 6,800 committed to the action. The Germans now considered the Australians as their most formidable adversaries.

For the first time the Allies were in a position to launch co-ordinated offensives on chosen segments of the Western Front. The French and Americans, the latter being switched in remarkably short time from St Mihiel, assaulted the German line in the Argonne on 26 September, and a long, hard slog it

proved to be. The next day the British were to go in towards Cambrai and on 28 September the armies in Flanders were to attack. On 29 September the Siegfried Position was to be the target.

The approach to Cambrai was barred by the Canal du Nord, a half-finished construction still waterless in places. To the east marshy land gave way to hills from which the Germans could observe and lay down fire. This daunting situation was to be faced by the Canadian Corps. Currie, its commander, selected the dry section of the canal to the south for his attack, planning to pass two divisions through the gap he intended to make and then spread them out beyond while pushing a third division through in support. Only sixteen tanks could be provided to him, so the artillery plans had to be precise and excellently managed. More than 1,000 aircraft were to support the attack, dropping 700 tons of bombs and firing some 26,000 rounds from their machine-guns. It was a scheme of a sophistication that could scarcely have been contemplated even a year earlier.

It worked perfectly. At 5.30am on 27 September the action started, and at the day's end the Canadians had taken all their objectives and more. German resistance was ferocious, but by the end of the second day the advance had penetrated six miles on a twelve-mile front. But fatigue slowly overcame the offensive; 1 October saw a further advance of only a mile. Another 7,000 prisoners and 205 guns were added to the Allies' trophies of war.

Now it was the turn of the main Siegfried Position to benefit from the Allies' attentions. Here the German defences made use of the St Quentin Canal, which curves around the town from the east to Bellenglise (34), then it heads north to Riqueval (16) to enter a tunnel under Bellicourt (10) and Bony before coming into the open once more to make its way towards Cambrai. South of the tunnel it passes through a deep cutting (16–22), which was fortified with concrete pillboxes and barbed-wire entanglements on the banks and in the canal itself. Closer to St Quentin it was almost waterless, but still full of mud. Evidently the open country over the tunnel

Above: German prisoners help with the recovery of casualties at the unfinished Canal du Nord. (TM 74/G1)

Right: The Hindenburg Line from Bellicourt to Bellenglise from the map of A. J. Gurr, B Company, 6th Tank Battalion. German trenches are in blue as at 19 September 1918 and the British front line is marked in blue pencil at a later date, probably immediately prior to the attack of 29 September. (TM Accu 442.6/8[3]. OS 62C N.E. & S.E. and 62B)

was the only place tanks could be of use, but here the depth of the defences was greatest, and in this sector Fourth Army was still well to the west (close to the line now followed by the A26 autoroute).

Once more Monash and the Australian Army Corps were given the tough assignment of breaking the German line above the tunnel. By now, however, they were deeply fatigued and short of men. The 1st and 4th Divisions were withdrawn from the line and replaced by the fresh, though inexperienced, American 27th and 30th Divisions under General George W. Read. They, with eighty-six tanks, were to overcome the German forward positions and the Australians, with seventy-six tanks, would pass through them to smash through the main line. An attempt was made to compensate for the lack of American combat knowledge by seconding 200 Australian officers and NCOs to them, but it was a dangerously optimistic arrangement. An additional proposal was submitted to Rawlinson by Lieutenant-General Sir Walter Braithwaite, commanding IX Corps, for an assault further south by the 46th (North Midland) Division with the 32nd Division in support, and this was added to the battle plan.

At 5.30am on 27 September the 106th Regiment of the American 27th Division went into action. The confusion of the battle is matched by the confusion of the historians; exactly what happened is uncertain. The Americans pressed forward and took at least the most advanced of the enemy positions. Individual acts of bravery such as Lieutenant William Bradford Turner's taking of two machinegun posts and leading his men in the crossing of four trenches were not enough. Turner lost his life, and was posthumously awarded the Congressional Medal of Honor, America's highest gallantry award. German counter-attacks regained those strongpoints that had been lost and by the end of the day the Americans had sustained 1,540 casualties. The next attack, two days later, now faced a ghastly problem. With an unknown number of their own troops out in front, should the attack have the support of a bombardment that might fall on their comrades? On 29 September the 27th went in once more, but without a creeping barrage.

In the dense fog confusion reigned again. When the Australians came up they found the Americans still valiantly fighting to take their objectives. The tanks failed to provide the answer; faced now with more flexible German tactics in the use of field artillery and anti-tank rifles, more than half of them were immobilized. The American 30th Division was in action also, and was equally mauled. By the afternoon the Australians pushing forward found themselves accompanied by Americans unwilling to give

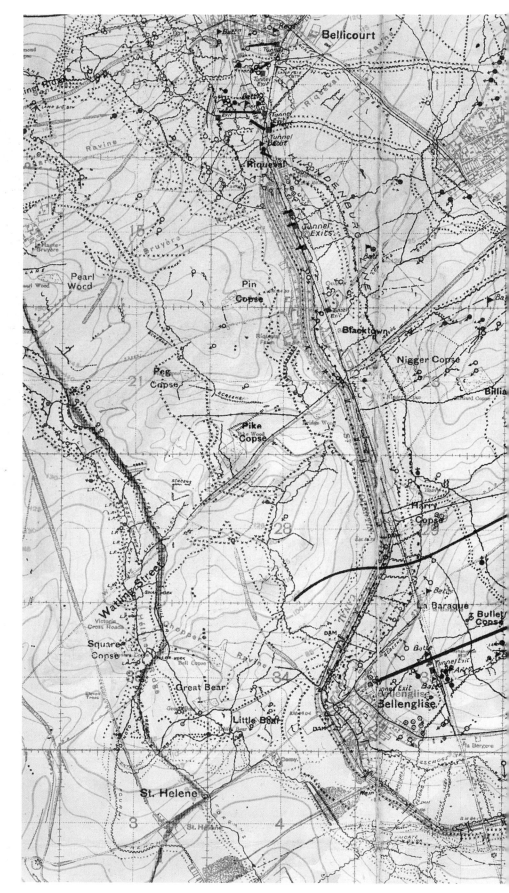

up and rejoin their own units, so they went on together, but still had not reached their final objectives when darkness fell. The 30th Division took 1,881 casualties, and by the time the battle waned three days later the Australians had suffered 1,500.

BELLENGLISE AND RIQUEVAL

The attempt to break the Hindenburg Line at Bony and Bellicourt had failed, but on 29 September that was not the only attack in progress. Formidable though the obstacle might be, a steep-sided, man-made gorge, extensive plans had been made to master the St Quentin Canal. This task fell to the

Territorials of 46th (North Midland) Division.

The Royal Engineers devised a series of gadgets. Mud mats of canvas and reeds were to provide footing over the miry shallows, ladders would be available to scale the steep canal banks, and collapsible boats would ferry troops across. The cross-Channel steamers were plundered of their life jackets. Experiment showed that a fully armed and equipped man could rely on a life jacket to keep him afloat and that the boats could be unfolded and on the water in 20 seconds. Such tests were not only prudent and practical, but excellent for morale.

As the Americans launched themselves against the line to the north, the 1/6th South Staffordshire Regiment advanced behind a creeping barrage from the positions secured by the division's 138 Brigade two days earlier. In the fog, and organized into small groups, they worked their way up to the enemy posi-

Left: Brigadier-General J. V. Campbell, VC, CMG, DSO, on the Riqueval Bridge, addressing men of 137 (Staffordshire) Brigade who had taken it in the morning fog on 29 September 1918. (P)

Above: Riqueval Bridge stands high above the Canal St Quentin, the banks of which are now thickly clad with trees. Without the bridge the Staffordshires would have faced an almost impossible obstacle. (MFME HS5/4)

tions then rushed in with the bayonet. The west bank was soon in their hands and they waded across to overwhelm the allegedly impregnable positions opposite. By 8.30am Bellenglise (34) was in their hands. On their left the 1/5th South Staffords made use of the boats to cross the waterway, also exploiting the advantage of the poor visibility.

Close to the southern end of the tunnel the Riqueval bridge (22) strides over the canal opposite the junction with the Le Cateau road (Watling Street to the British) to give the local farmers access to the fields on the western bank. The Germans had, of course, prepared charges so that it could be blown up in the event of an attack.

In the fog of the morning of 29 September, Captain A. H. Charlton had to navigate by compass to find the bridge at all. As his company of the 1/6th North Staffords emerged from the mist they came under fire from a machine-gun sited in a trench on the western side. A bayonet charge put an end to that. Alerted by the firing, the demolition party of four men appeared from the German bunker beyond the bridge and ran to blow the charges fixed to the structure. Charlton and his men beat them to it, killing all four and cutting the wires to the explo-

sives. The rest of the company dashed over the bridge and cleared the trenches and bunkers to secure passage for the brigade.

The supporting troops moved up and through the successful assault force to continue the advance. To the rear the fog persisted, causing confusion amongst units attempting to move up and great difficulties for those wounded seeking the dressing stations behind the line. The tanks became targets as the fog dispersed in front, but the advance continued and great columns of German prisoners began their journeys to the cages. By the time, early in the afternoon, that the commanders could see clearly they were rewarded with the most heartening sight of this long war, a genuine breakthrough.

The 46th Division took 4,200 prisoners that day, 80 per cent of the total to fall into Allied hands in this sector. They had done this at the cost of fewer than 800 casualties. But most remarkable of all, against the strongest defensive system the Germans had been able to construct, they had advanced nearly three and a half miles.

In the days following the momentum was maintained. On 3 October Fourth Army broke through the Beaurevoir Line, and on the 5th the 49th (West

Above: In spite of increasing mechanization the progress of armies was limited by the fatigue of foot soldiers. (P)

Riding) Division and the Australian 2nd Division took Ramicourt and Montbréhain, to the right of the Le Cateau road, to complete the conquest of the Siegfried Position. The entire Hindenburg Line had been broken. Ahead lay green fields and unblemished countryside, and an enemy now doomed to defeat.

THE FINAL WEEKS

For Germany, the need to sue for an armistice was now undeniable. Amidst growing political instability a new administration under Prince Max of Baden took power in Germany. As the events of the next few weeks unfolded the unity and reliability of the German armed forces crumbled, but the army remained a serious adversary and the Allies still had hard fighting before them. In the east the French and the Americans battled on in the Argonne and in Champagne. In the north September had seen the Germans rolled back in Flanders. On 14 October the last shell fell on Ypres and, two days later, the British occupied Menin, some ten miles to the east, and slightly south, of Ypres, a town that had been

their objective four years before.

Beyond the Hindenburg Line the open, undamaged landscape appealed to enthusiasts of wars of movement; it looked perfect for cavalry or tank deployment. The efforts of the cavalry were, for the most part, futile, however, since the machine-gun still dominated the field in close action. As for tanks,

Above: The evacuation of French wounded by canal boat. (HGG)

Left: American infantrymen of the 308th Regiment take a rest after capturing a German trench in the Argonne Forest. (NA 111SC 22343)

there were scarcely any of them left – but, more important, the Tank Corps had lost approximately one-third of its men, and skilled, well-trained specialists were required for these weapons. The speed of advance thus depended, as always, on the infantry, and on the army's ability to supply them. The supplies, of course, had to be brought up over that very country for which the armies had fought for the last four years: along shattered roads and through tortured and denuded fields, past heaps of stone where once villages had stood, through the few stumps which indicated that here once was a wood. Finally, the troops themselves found the environment strange. After years of closely controlled action over distances measured in tens of yards, they were unprepared for the demands of open warfare.

Although these factors slowed the advance, and although German resistance persisted in the face of defeat, the advance continued. Lille fell on 17 October and Douai on the same day. On 17 October the Fourth Army was fighting on the River Selle, northeast of Cambrai, in worsening weather. In three days

they took 5,000 prisoners. On the same day Le Cateau, scene of the noted rearguard action by the British in 1914, was liberated.

The last of the Bushmills men to die in that war was killed on 4 November. Joseph Thompson had emigrated to New Zealand in 1913 to join his brother. Both of them enlisted, and Joseph became a lance-corporal in the New Zealand Rifle Brigade. He was going forward with the medical officer and the chaplain to establish a regimental aid post on the road from Romeries to Le Quesnoy, east of Cambrai, at about 8am when a machine-gun opened fire. They took cover, but Thompson had been hit. The chaplain buried him nearby later that day.

In Germany the Kaiser refused to recognize the extreme seriousness of the situation. Ordered to sea, the German High Seas Fleet mutinied. On 7 November Secretary of State Matthias Erzberger led the delegation to meet Foch in a railway carriage ner Compiègne to negotiate an armistice. Two days later the Kaiser abdicated and fled to the Netherlands. Revolution gripped Berlin. All attempts to extract more favourable terms from the Allies failed and on 10 November Erzberger received news from Berlin

Left: German medics treat wounded British troops near Bapaume. (P)

Above: Walking wounded pass patient stretcher cases while exhausted stretcher-bearers pause for rest. (TM)

that the conditions prescribed had been accepted. At ten minutes past five on the morning of 11 November the document was signed. Foch immediately issued instructions to his forces to cease operations at 11 o'clock.

On 11 November the Canadians were at a scene of a famous action in 1914 – Mons. One of their number, Private Price, was shot dead at 10.58am. At 11am the guns fell silent at last.

Today countless people speed along the autoroutes from Calais to Reims and from Lille to Paris. If they can spare a second or two to glance at the countryside they may catch a glimpse of a cemetery or see some unidentified monument silhouetted against the sky. They give no thought to the thousands who suffered and died here. For those who take the slower country roads the evidence of sacrifice is more easily discovered, and those who choose to walk in the footsteps of the brave will find memories more resonant than words can describe.

The literature of the Somme is extensive, and that of the First World War vast. In the preparation of this book I have consulted and, on occasion, quoted from, the works listed below. The list does not pretend to be more than a personal one.

Anon., *The Western Front Then and Now*, London, C. Arthur Pearson, 1938.

Audouin-Rouzeau, Stéphane, *Men at War 1914–1918*, Oxford, Berg, 1992.

Banks, Arthur, *A Military Atlas of the First World War*, London, Leo Cooper, 1989.

Brown, Malcolm, *The Imperial War Museum Book of the First World War*, London, Sidgwick & Jackson, 1991.

Chappell, Michael, *The Somme 1916: Crucible of a British Army*, London, Windrow & Greene, 1995.

Farndale, General Sir Martin, 'The Battle of Amiens, 1918', in David Chandler (ed.), *Great Battles of the British Army*, London, Arms and Armour, 1991.

Farrar-Hockley, General Sir Anthony, 'The Battle of the Somme; 1916', in David Chandler (ed.), *Great Battles of the British Army*, London, Arms and Armour, 1991.

Gilbert, Martin, *First World War*, London, Weidenfeld & Nicolson, 1994.

Gliddon, Gerald, *When the Barrage Lifts: A topographical history and commentary on the Battle of the Somme 1916*, Norwich, Gliddon Books, 1987.

Glover, Michael, *A New Guide to the Battlefields of Northern France and the Low Countries*, London, Michael Joseph, 1987.

Holt, Tonie and Valmai, *Battlefields of the First World War*, London, Pavilion, 1993.

Holt, Tonie and Valmai, *Battle Map of the Somme*, Sandwich, Holt's Battlefield Tours, 1995.

Liveing, Edward, *Attack on the Somme*, Stevenage, Spa/Tom Donovan Military Books, 1986.

Malins, Geoffrey, *How I Filmed the War*, London, Herbert Jenkins, 1920.

Macdonald, Lyn, *Somme*, London, Michael Joseph, 1983.

Masefield, John, ed. Peter Vansittart, *Letters from the Front 1915–17*, London, Constable, 1984.

McCarthy, Chris, *The Somme: The Day-By-Day Account*, London, Arms and Armour, 1993.

Middlebrook, Martin, *The First Day on the Somme*, London, Allen Lane, 1971.

Parker, Ernest, *Into Battle 1914–1918*, London, Longmans, Green, 1964.

Sheffield, G. D., *The Pictorial History of World War I*, London, Bison Books, 1987.

Simkins, Peter, *Kitchener's Army: The Raising of the New Armies, 1914–16*, Manchester, Manchester University Press, 1988.

Simkins, Peter, *World War 1 1914–1918: The Western Front*, Godalming, CLB Publishing, 1991.

Terraine, John, *To Win a War: 1918, The Year of Victory*, London, Macmillan, 1986.

Thompson, Robert (ed.), *Bushmills Heroes 1914–1918*, Bushmills (Co. Antrim), Thompson, 1995.

Vaughan, Edwin Campion, *Some Desperate Glory*, London, Frederick Warne, 1981.

Westlake, Ray, *British Battalions on the Somme: Battles and engagements of the 616 infantry battalions involved in the Battle of the Somme*, London, Leo Cooper, 1994.

Their name liveth for evermore

Flat Iron Copse Cemetery